Cayuga and York Ontario in Colour Photos, Saving Our History One Photo at a Time

Photography
by Barbara Raué
©2018

Series Name: Cruising Ontario

Book 213: Cayuga, York

Cover photo: 1 Cayuga Street North

©All the photos in this book have been taken with my cameras. I own the rights to them.

Series Name: Cruising Ontario
Saving Our History One Photo at a Time
in colour photos

Books Available in Alphabetical Order:
Aberfoyle, Acton, Ajax, Alton, Amherstburg, Ancaster, Arthur, Auburn, Aylmer, Ayr, Beaver Valley, Belgrave, Belleville, Bloomingdale, Blyth, Brantford, Brockville, Burford, Burlington, Caledon, Caledonia, Cambridge, Carlow, Chatsworth, Clifford, Collingwood, Conestogo, Delhi, Dorchester to Aylmer, Drayton, Drumbo, Dundas, Dunlop, Eden Mills, Elmira, Elora, Erin, Essex, Fergus, Goderich, Grimsby, Guelph, Hagersville, Hamilton, Hanover, Harriston, Hespeler, Jarvis, Kingston, Kingsville, Kitchener, Lake Superior, Lincoln, Linwood, Listowel, London, Lucknow, Merrickville, Mono, Mount Forest, Mount Pleasant, Neustadt, New Hamburg, Newboro, Newport, Niagara-on-the-Lake, Niagara Falls, North Bay, Oakville, Onondaga, Orangeville, Orillia, Oshawa, Owen Sound, Palmerston, Paris, Pelham, Perth, Peterborough, Petrolia, Pickering, Port Colborne, Port Elgin, Portland, Preston, Rockwood, Sarnia, Sault Ste. Marie, Seaforth, Sheffield, Shelburne, Simcoe, Smiths Falls, Smithville, Southampton, St. Catharines, St. George, St. Jacobs, St. Marys, St. Thomas, Stoney Creek, Stratford, Thamesford, Thunder Bay, Tillsonburg, Toronto, Waterdown, Waterford, Waterloo, Welland, Wellesley, West Flamborough, Westport, Whitby, Windsor, Wingham, Woodstock

Book 207-209: Niagara Falls
Book 210: North Bay
Book 211: Fort Erie
Book 212-215: Haldimand
    County

Early patterns of settlement in Haldimand County are still visible in the landscape and architecture, spanning from the pre-Contact era to the proclamation of the Haldimand Land Grant for the Six Nations and the subsequent migration of Loyalist settlers – Americans, largely of German descent and Mennonite tradition. Throughout the 1800s, immigration from the British Isles contributed significantly to the area's development, as did the small but industrious Black community of the late nineteenth century – many descended from ex-slaves of the American South. Since the post-war years of the twentieth century, a significant stream of immigration from the Netherlands has also added to our ever-expanding mosaic of cultural identity, as have the age-old traditions of our Indigenous neighbours – the Six Nations and New Credit communities.

Following the American Revolution, Sir Frederick Haldimand, Governor-in-Chief of Canada, granted in 1784 to the Six Nations of the Iroquois a tract of land extending for six miles on both sides of the Grand River from its source to Lake Erie. This grant was made in recognition of their services as allies of the British Crown during the war, and to recompense them for the loss of their former lands in northern New York State. In later years, large areas of this tract, including portions of the present counties of Haldimand, Brant, Waterloo and Wellington, were sold to white settlers.

By 1853, Cayuga had lumber yards, a foundry, and a glass factory.

At its height, York had twenty businesses that included mills, inns, shoemakers, general stores, blacksmiths, and a lumber yard. It had a two-room school house and two churches.

Cayuga

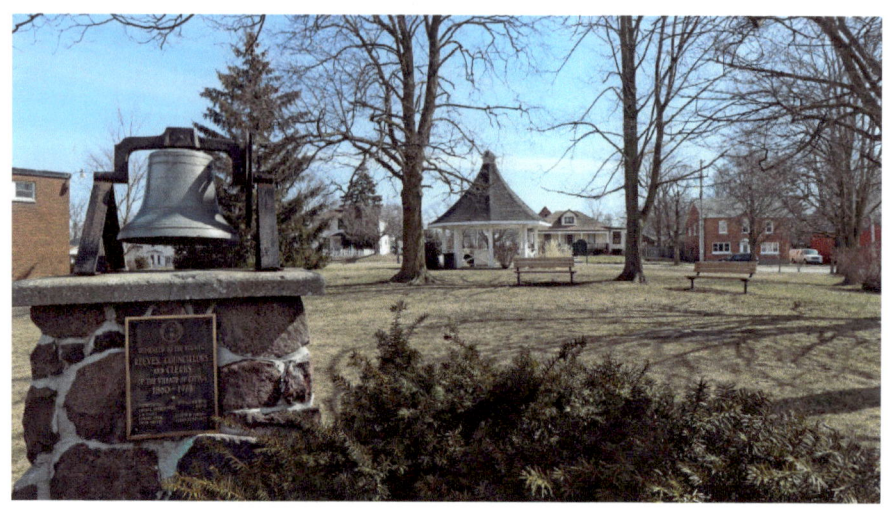

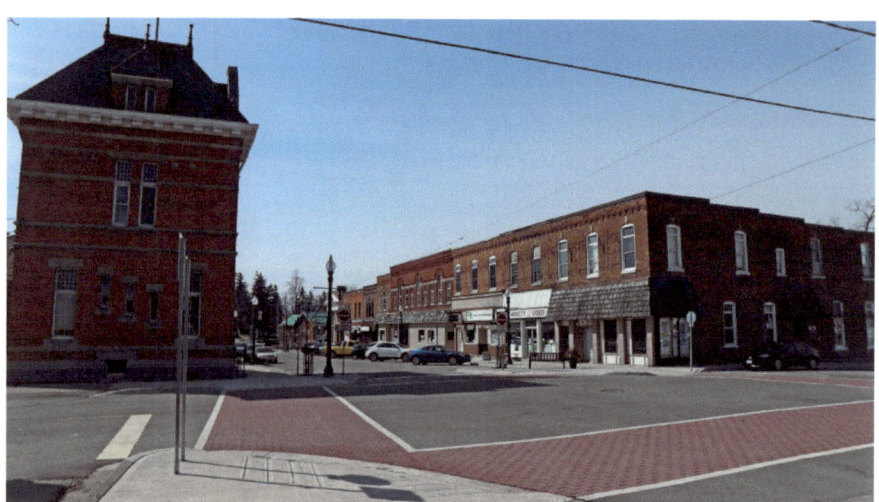

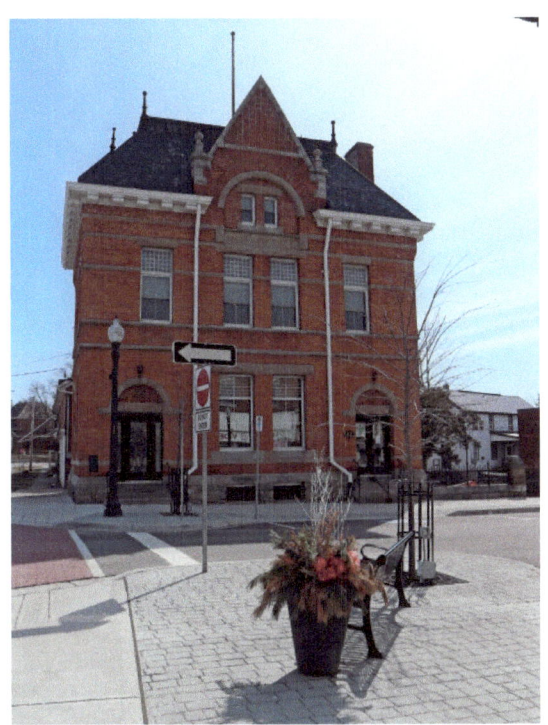

12 Cayuga Street North – Post Office

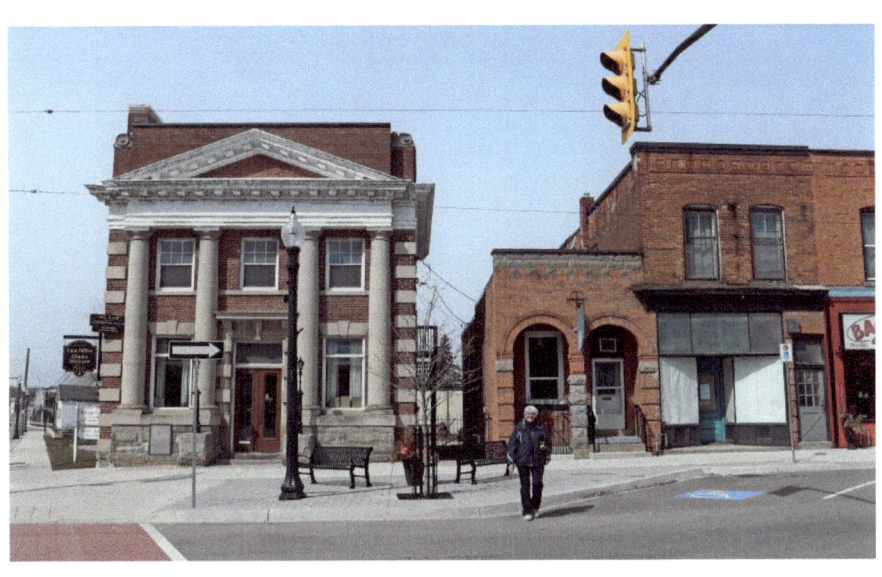

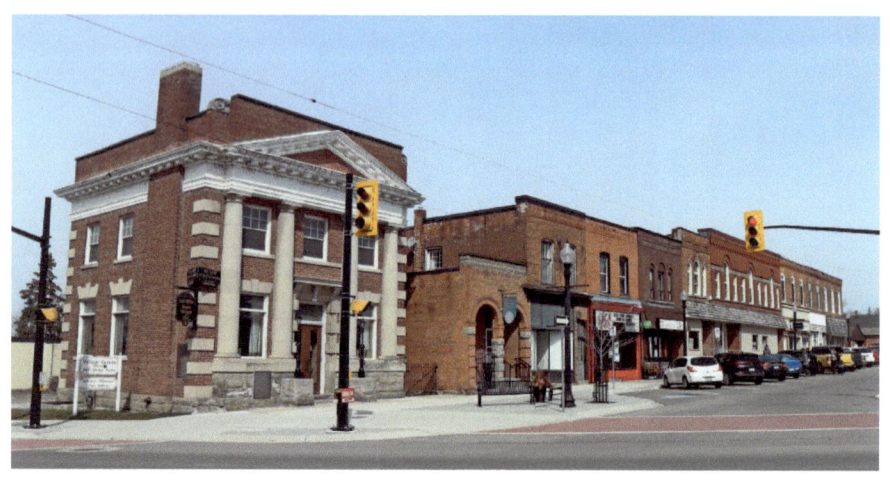

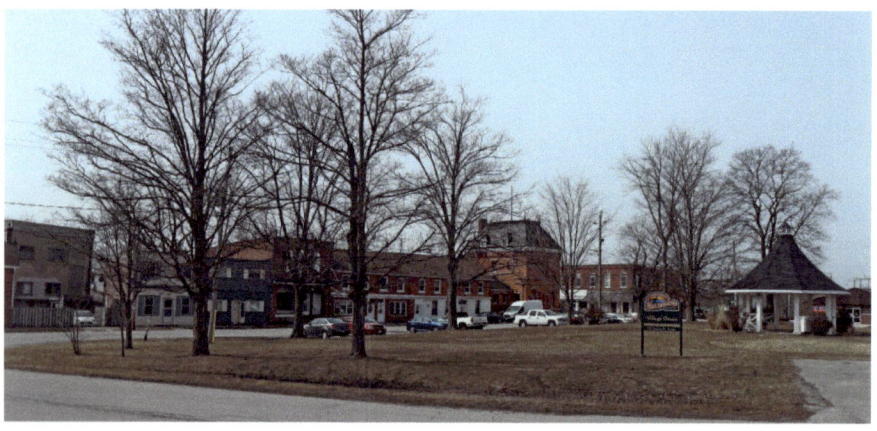

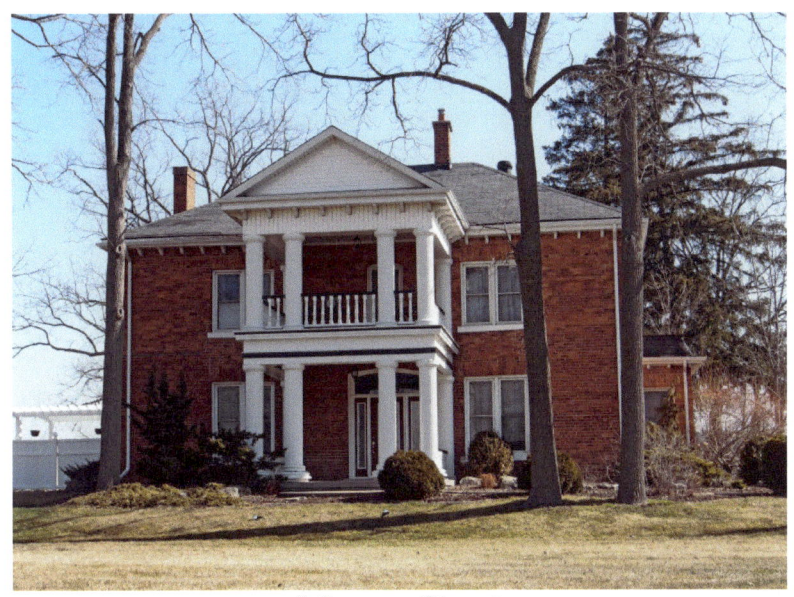
Munsee Street

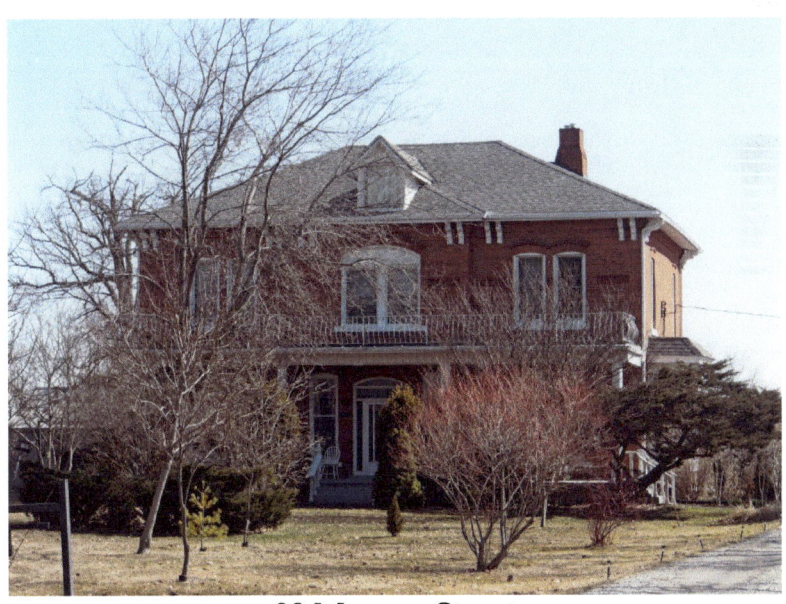
98 Munsee Street

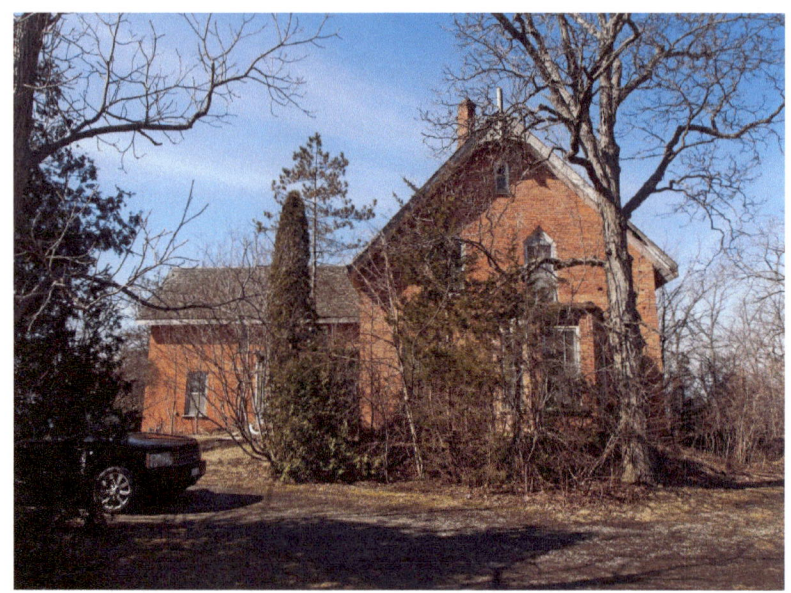

Munsee Street

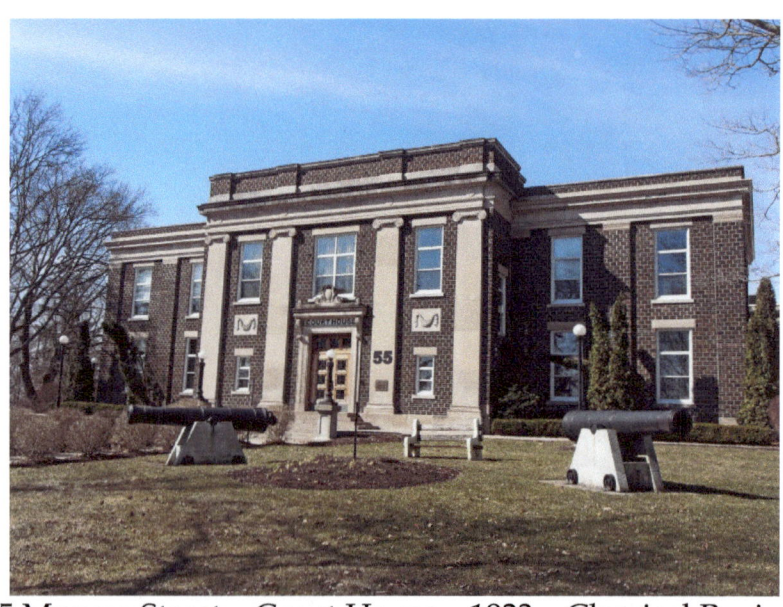

55 Munsee Street – Court House – 1923 – Classical Revival style of architecture - low hipped roof, pilasters

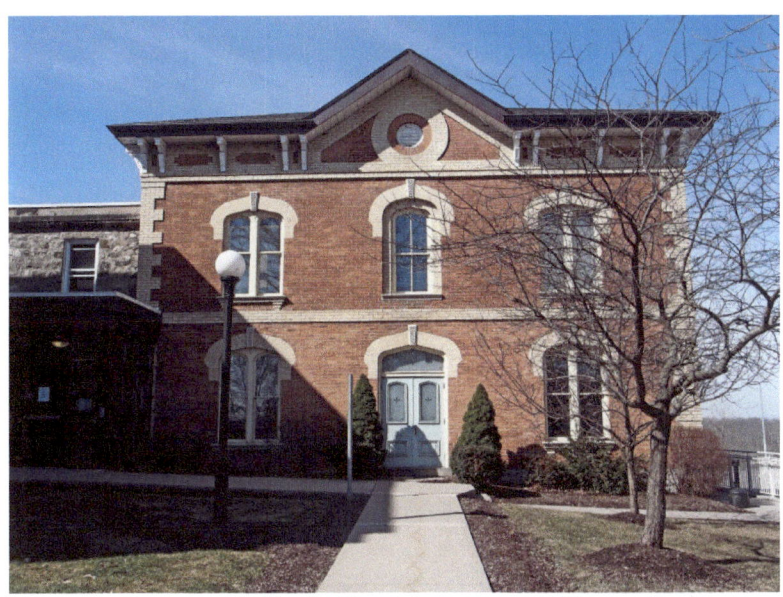

55 Munsee Street – Jailer's Residence – 1877 – Italianate style, low hipped roof, overhanging eaves with brackets, a bullseye window

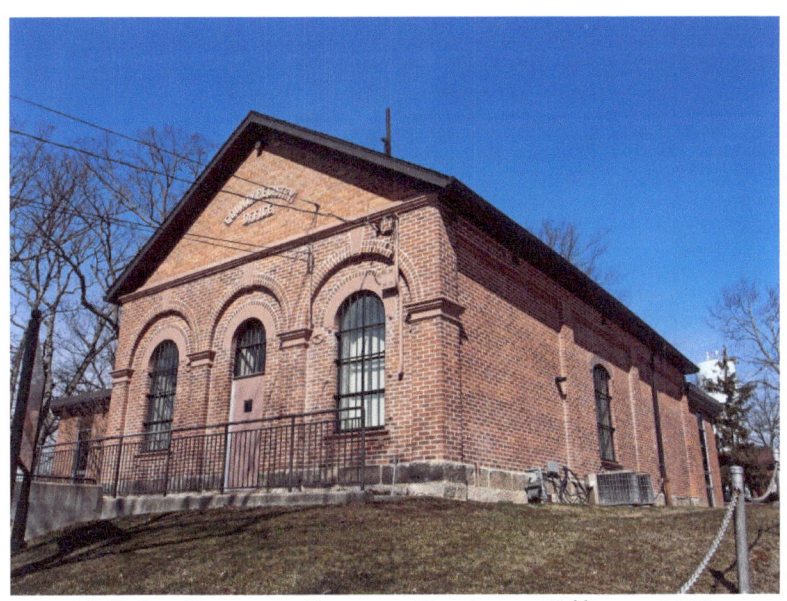

10 Echo Street – County Registry Office – 1871

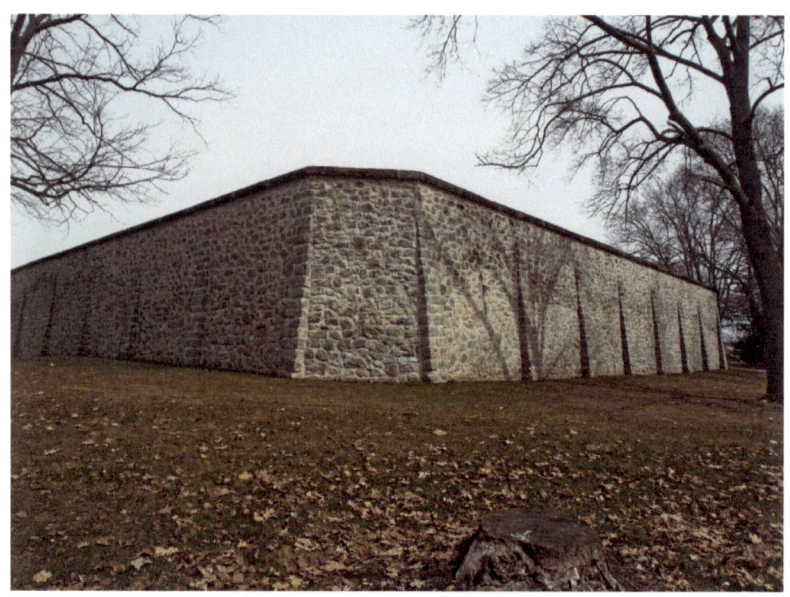
Stone jail – 1850-1851

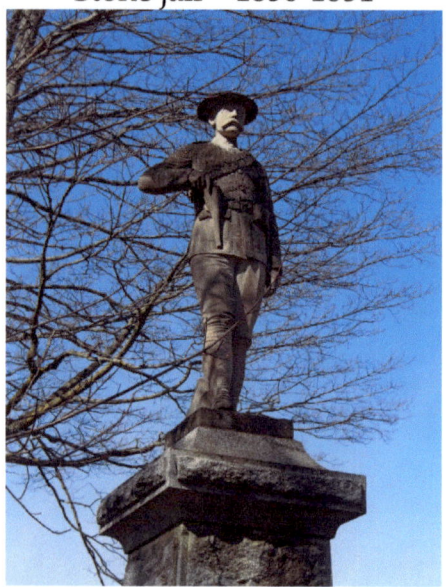
Munsee Street – Knisley Memorial – Corporal William A. Knisley, Royal Canadian Dragoons, was decorated with the Distinguished Conduct Medal for gallantry at Leliefontein and who gave his life at the Battle of Harts River, April 2, 1902 in the South African (Boer) War.

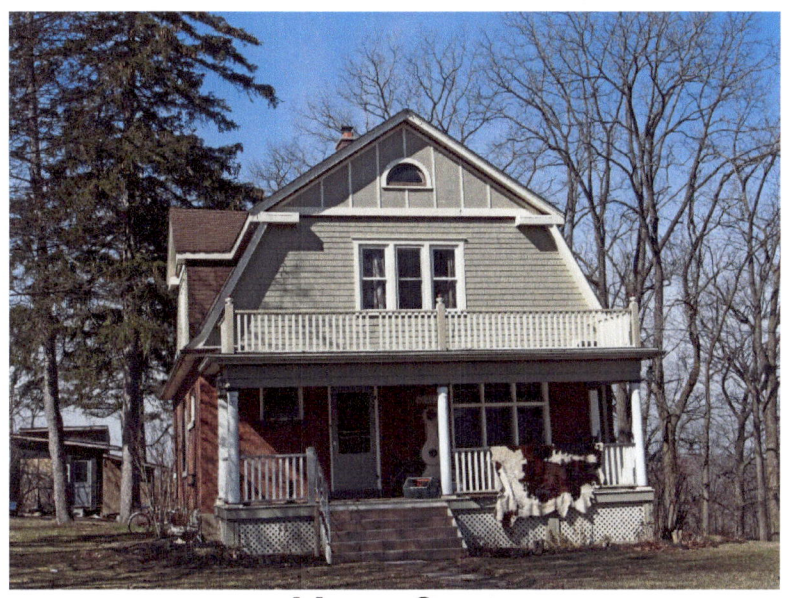

Munsee Street

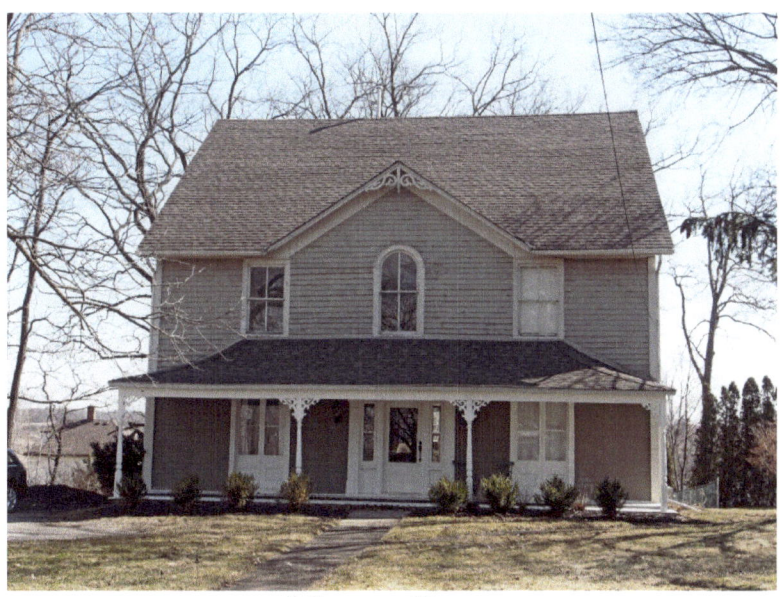

Munsee Street

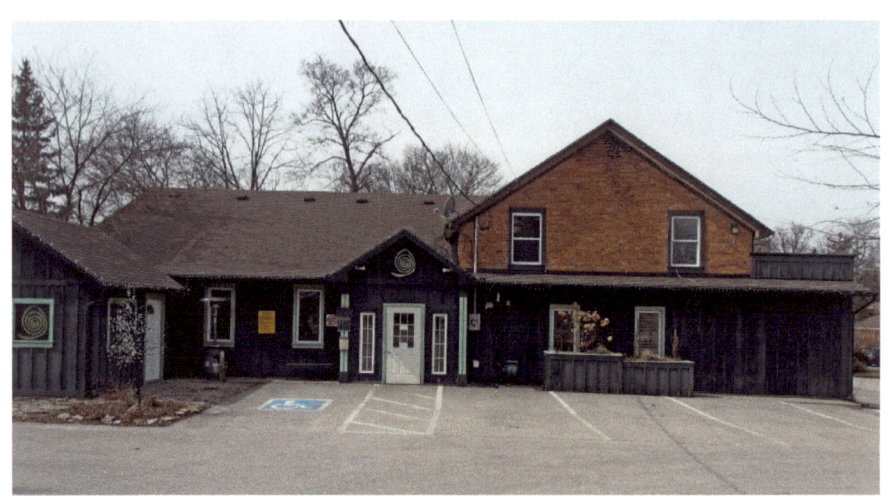
Munsee Street

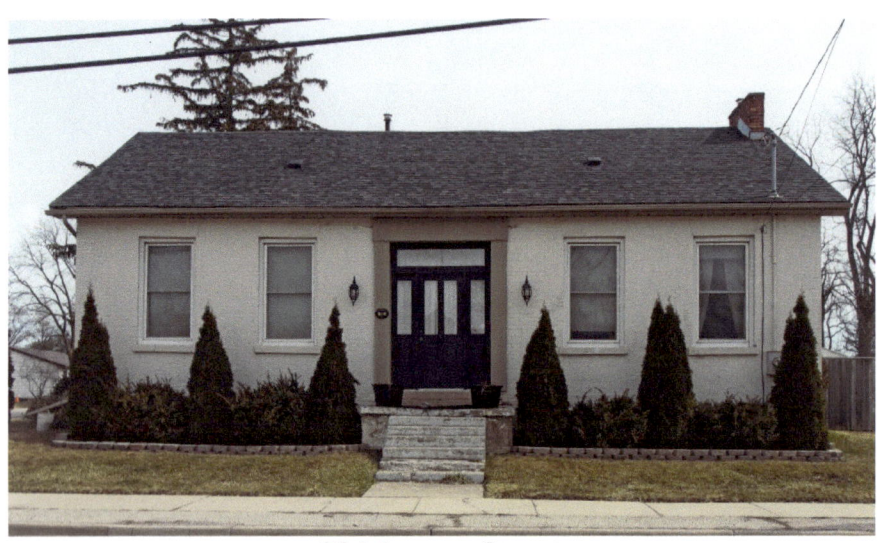
28 Munsee Street

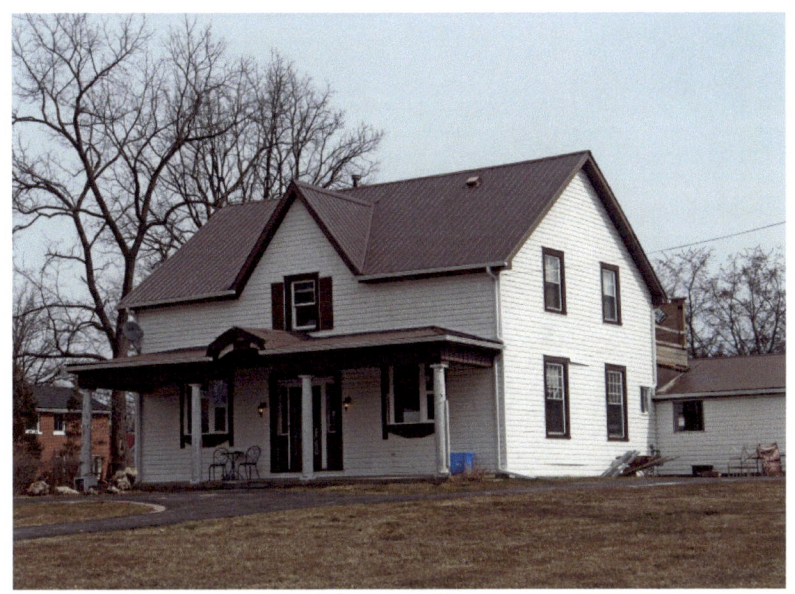

32 Munsee Street

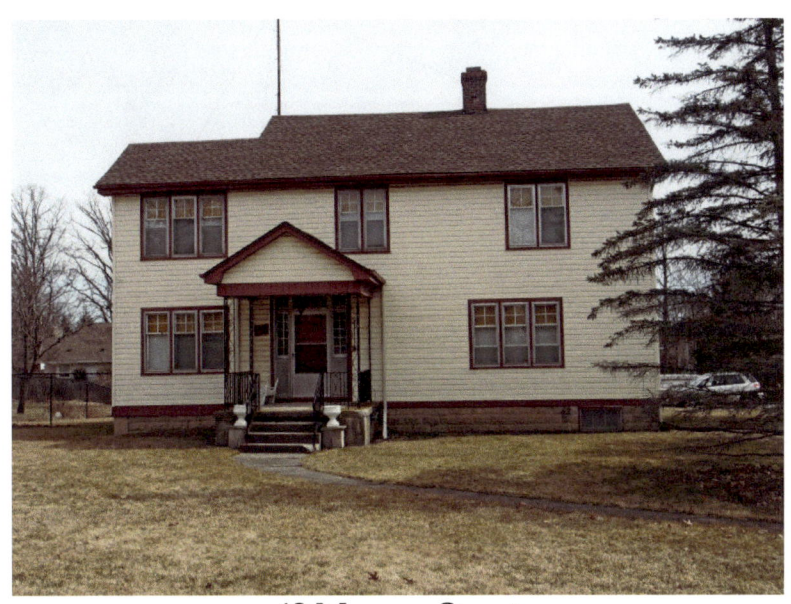

42 Munsee Street

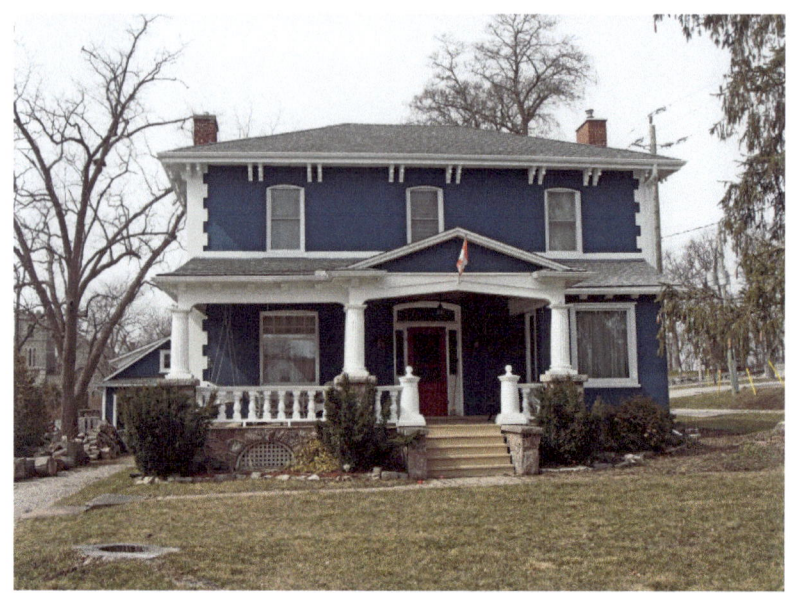

Munsee Street

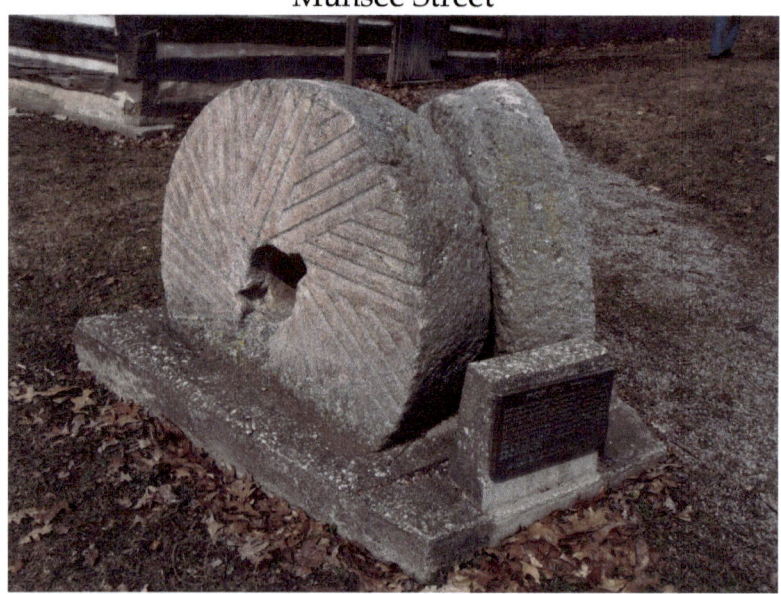

In 1811, Matthew W. Smith located the site for a flour and saw mill on the Dunnville Road, south of the village of Canborough. The mill was first operated by horses and later by water power.

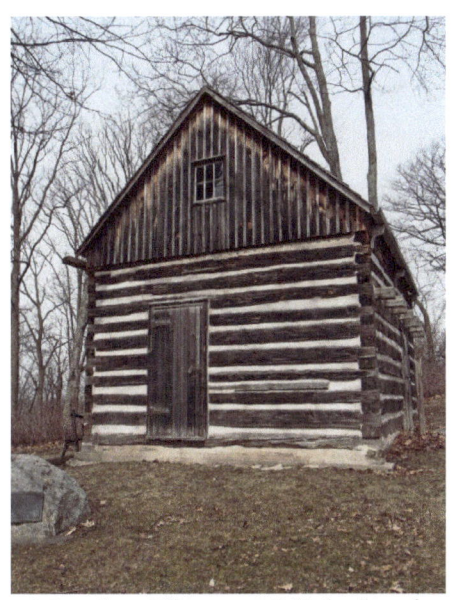

45 Munsee Street North – Thomas Nicholas from Fowery, Cornwall on the banks of the English Channel, built a log cabin about 1835 beside the Old Plank Road (Highway 6) south of Caledonia in the former Oneida Township. As his large family grew, a second story was added to the one room home. In 1961, the cabin and its artifacts were re-erected in Cayuga's Courthouse Park as part of the Haldimand County Museum and Archive. The gabled roof is covered by cedar shingles; the oak logs were hand-hewn and sand mortar was used.

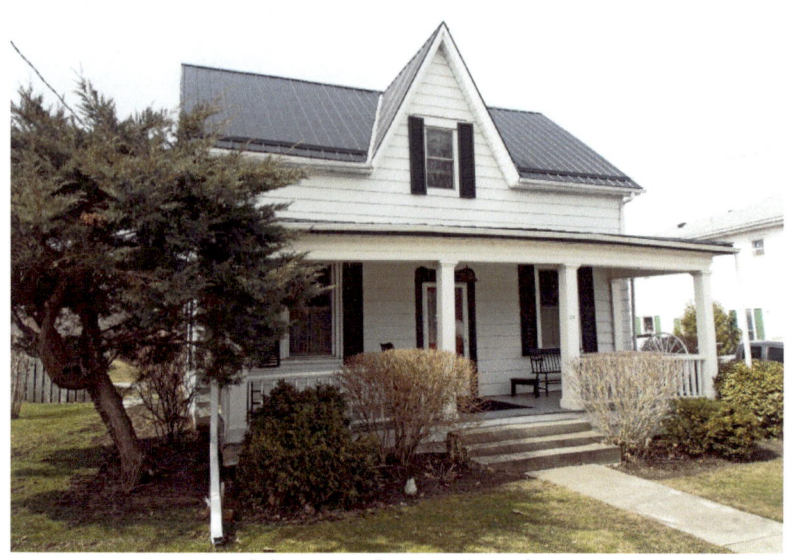

Munsee Street South

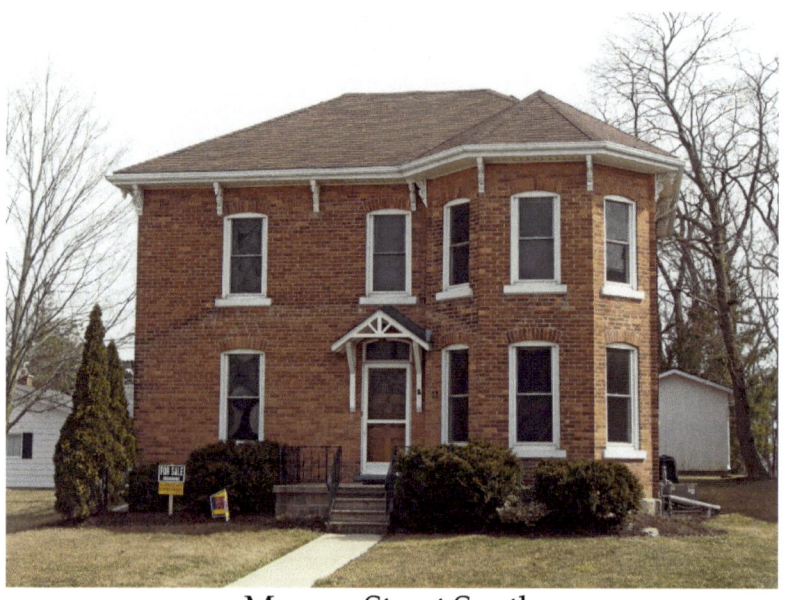

Munsee Street South

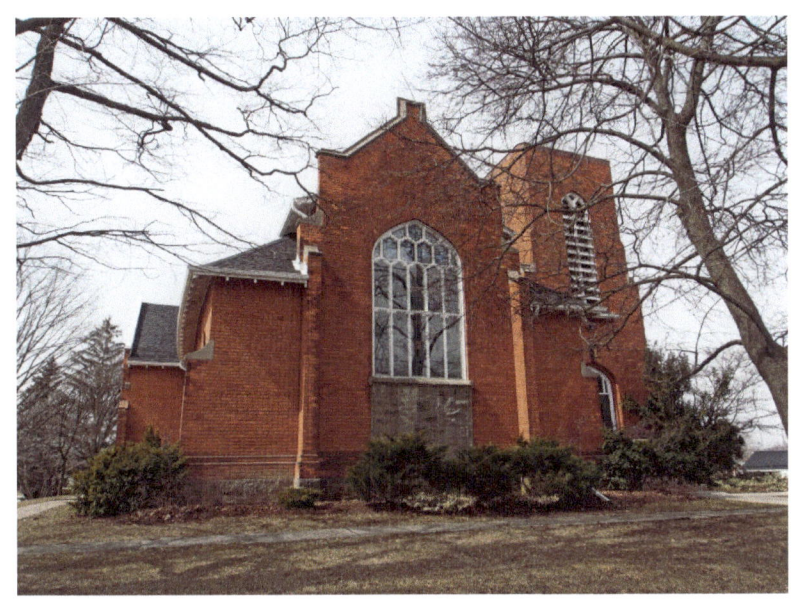

27 Munsee Street South – Cayuga United Church

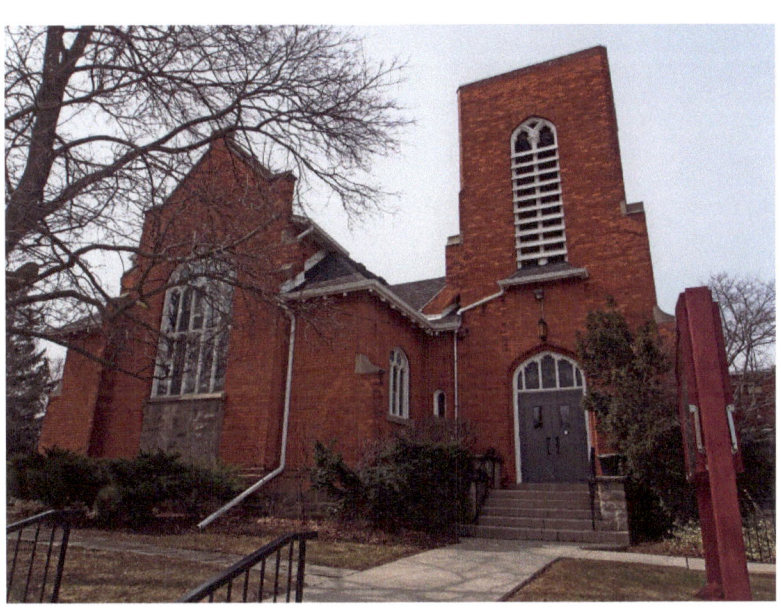

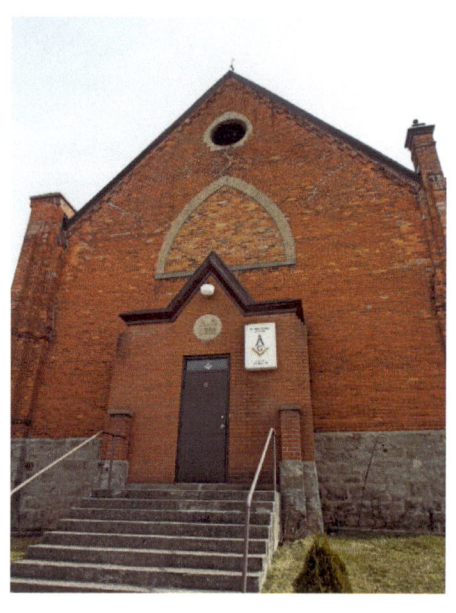

8 Munsee Street North – St. John's Lodge

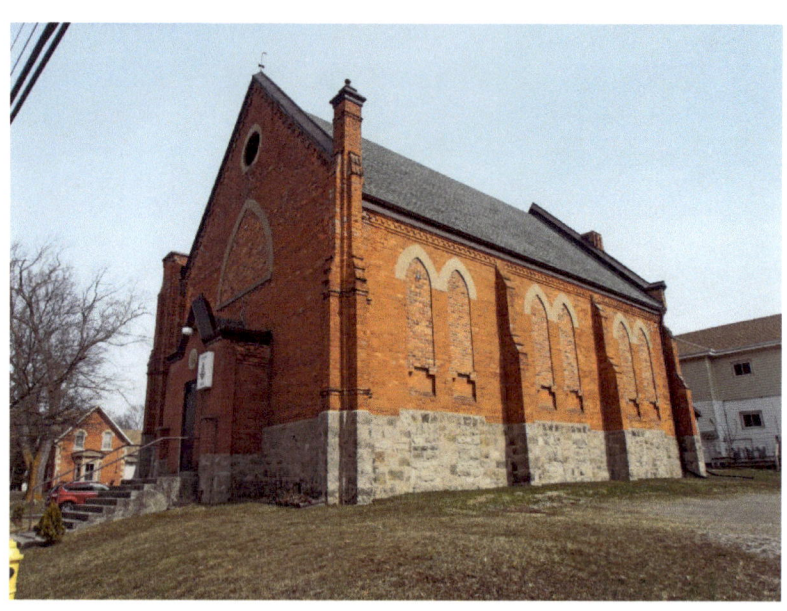

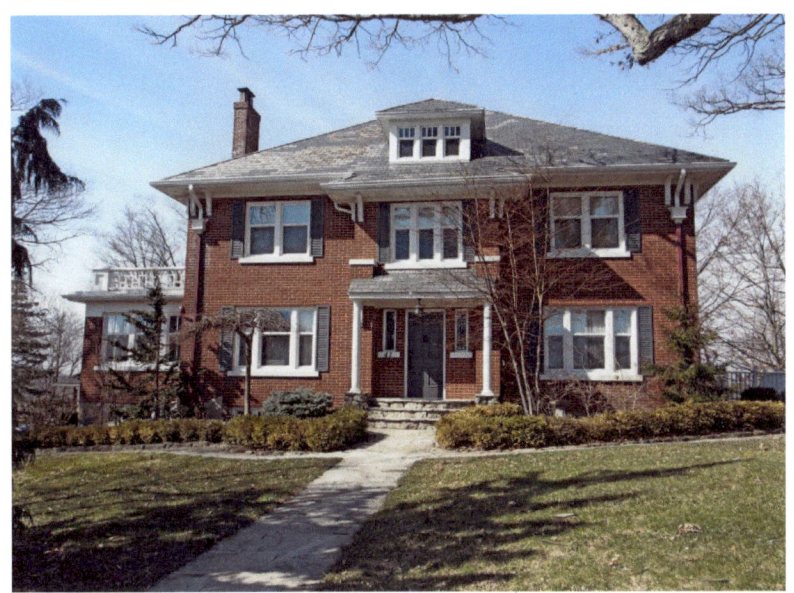
41 Echo Street

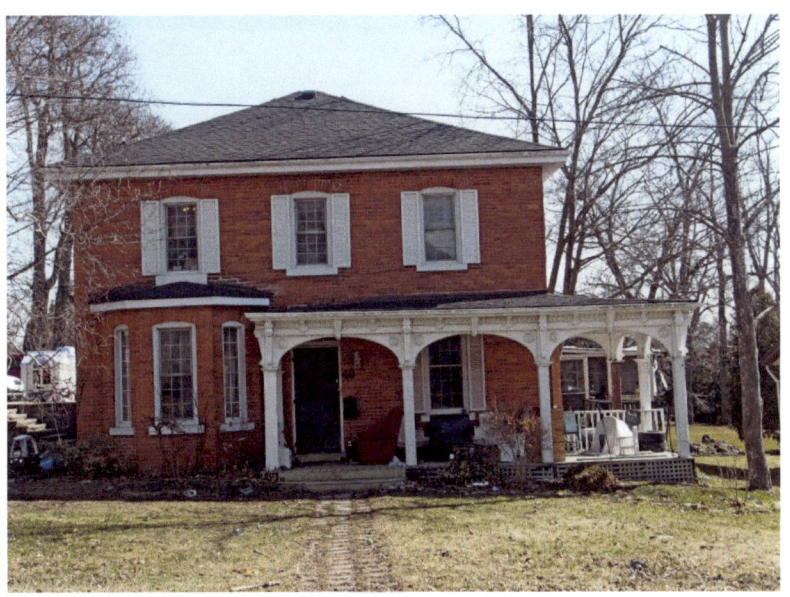
40 Ottawa Street

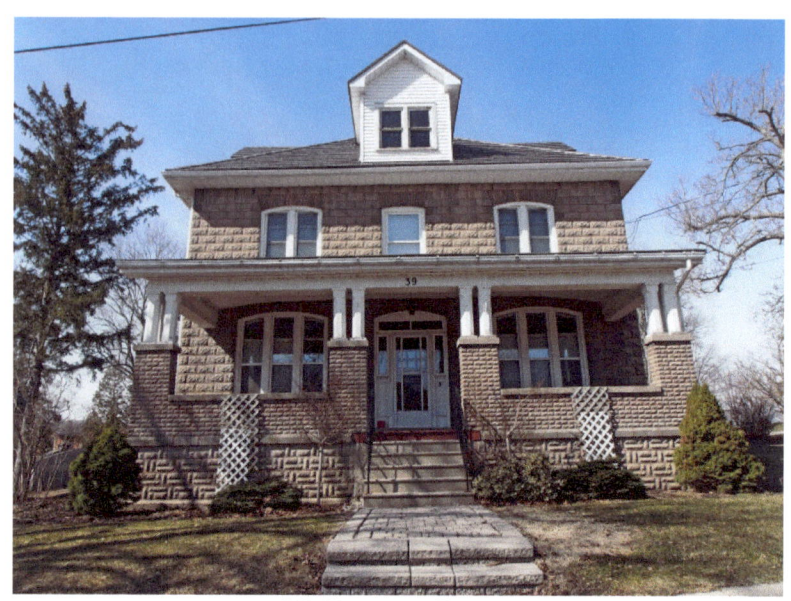

39 Ottawa Street

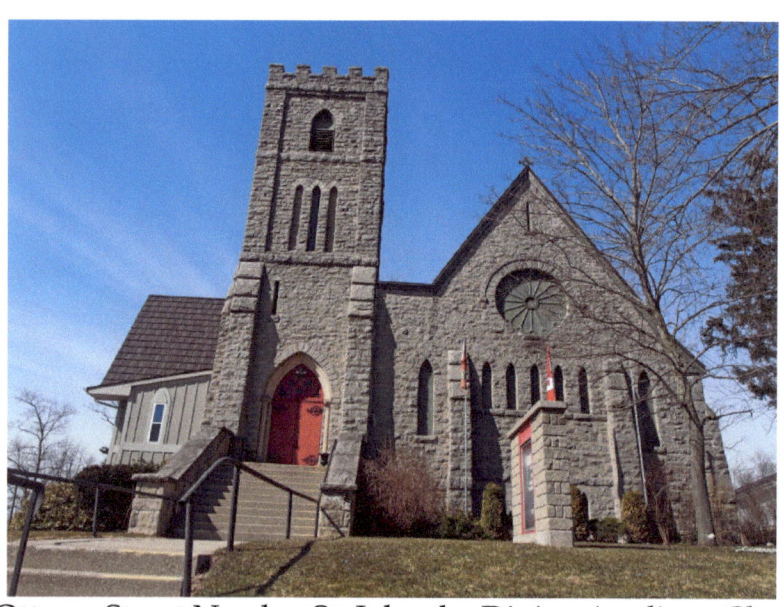

37 Ottawa Street North – St. John the Divine Anglican Church - 1896

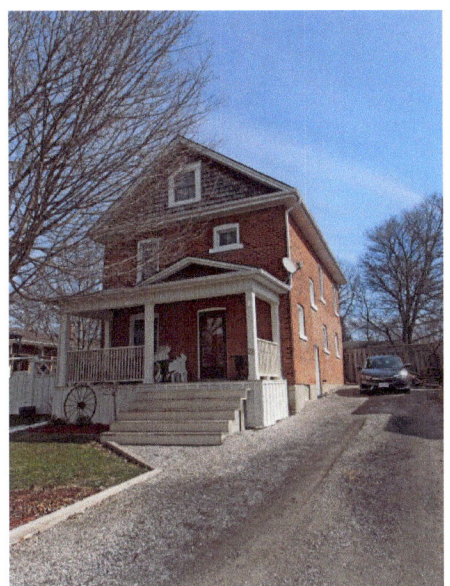

28 Ottawa Street

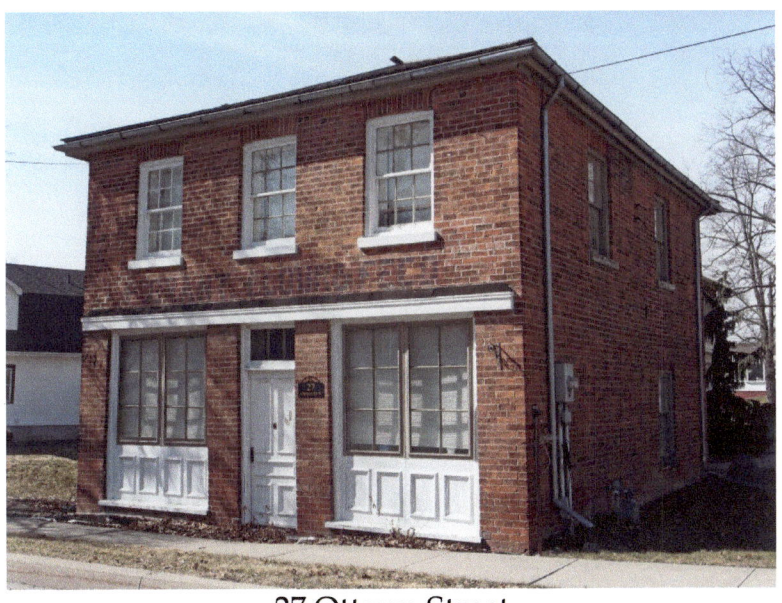

27 Ottawa Street

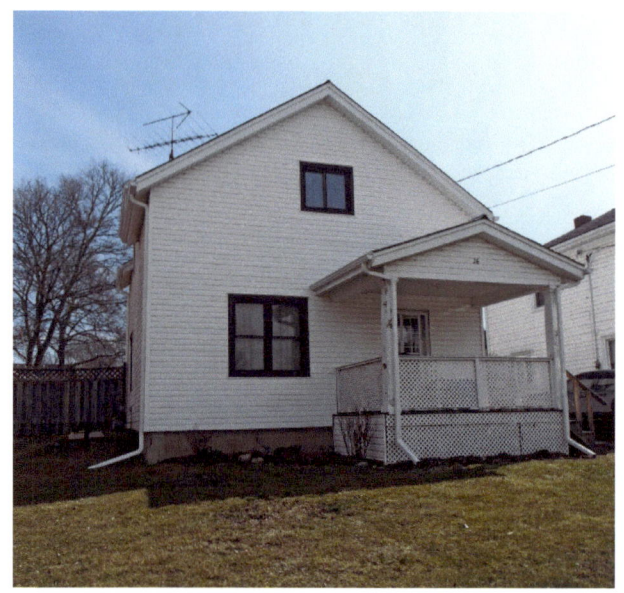

26 Ottawa Street

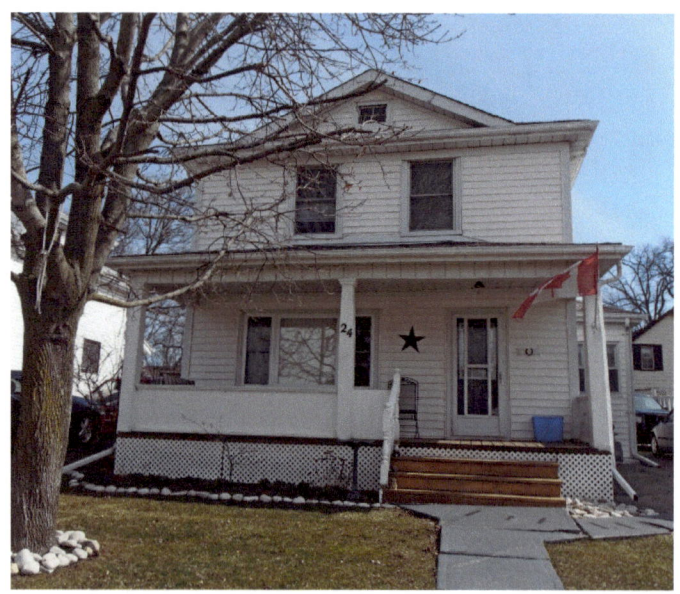

24 Ottawa Street

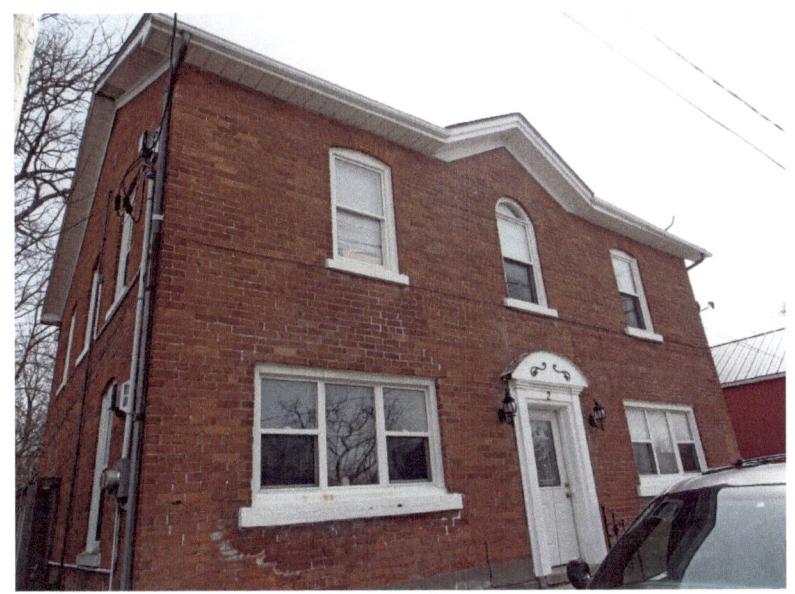

2 Ottawa Street

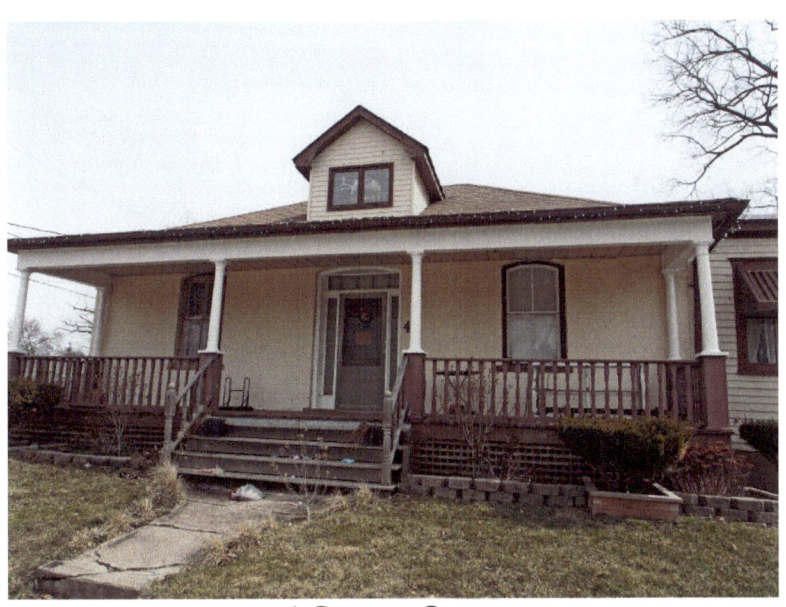

4 Ottawa Street

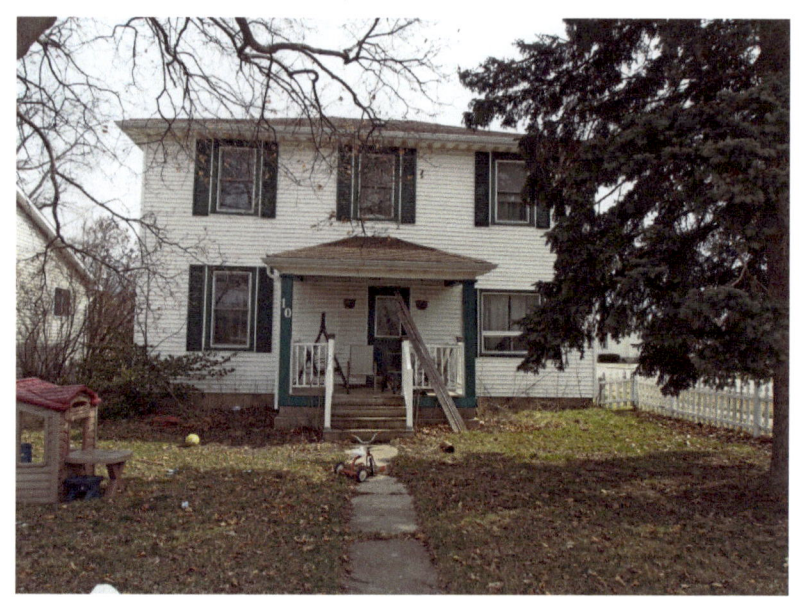

10 Ottawa Street

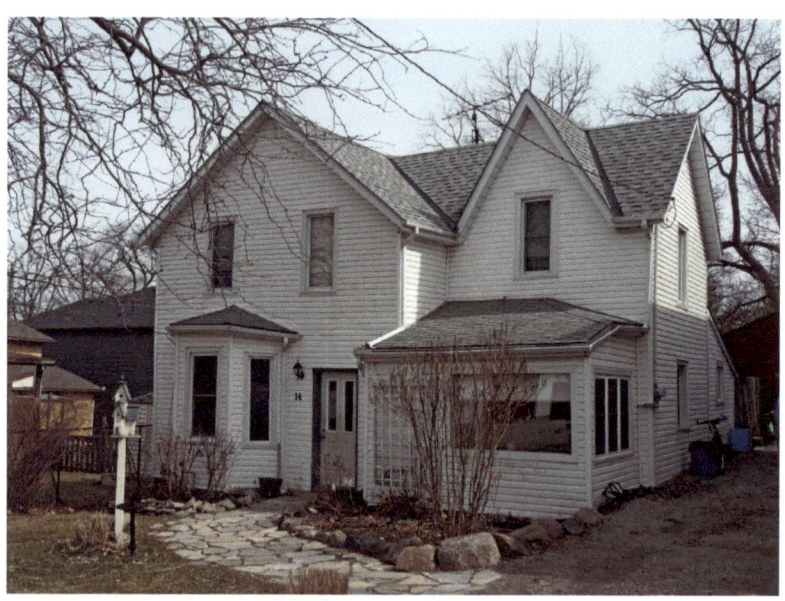

14 Ottawa Street

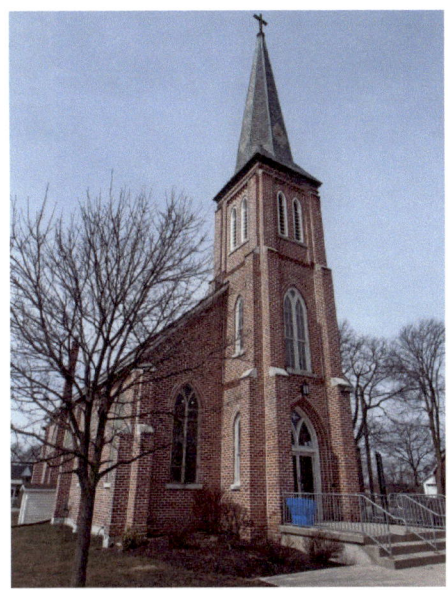
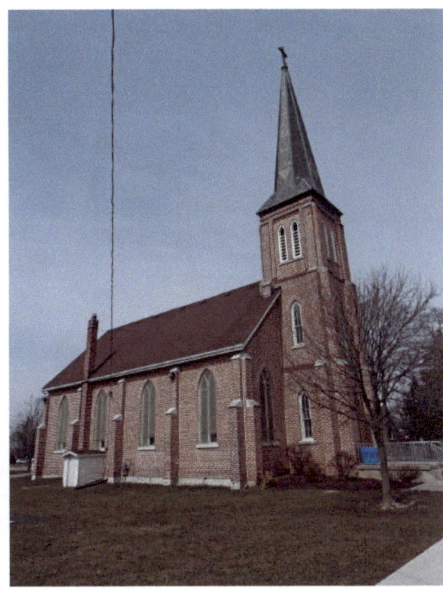

15 Ottawa Street South – St. Stephen's Roman Catholic Church

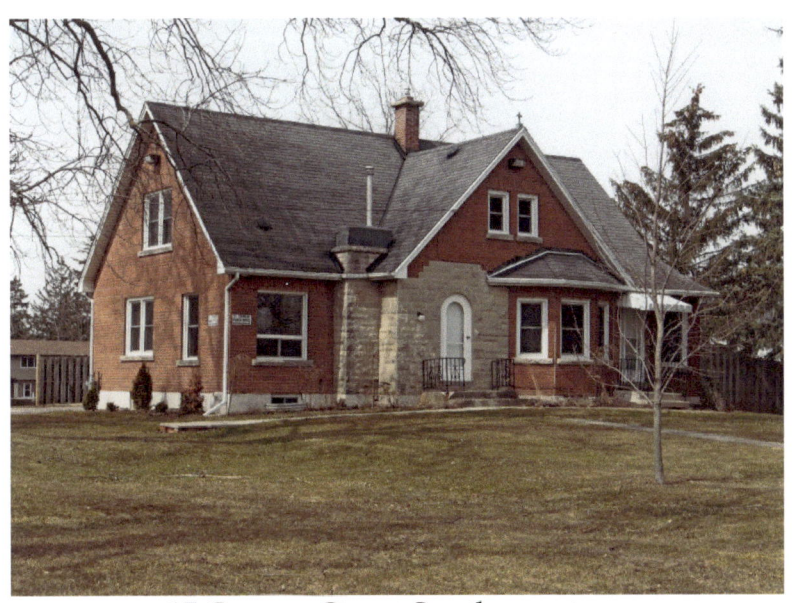

15 Ottawa Street South – rectory

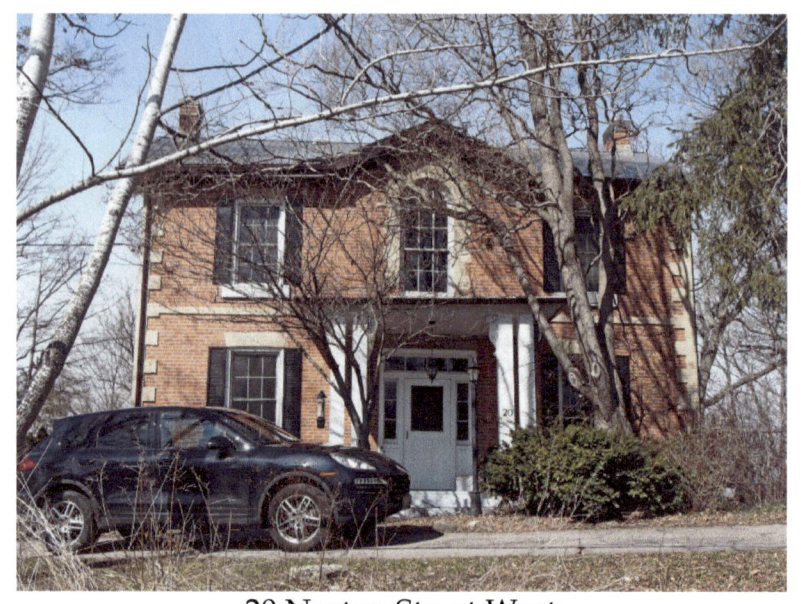
20 Norton Street West

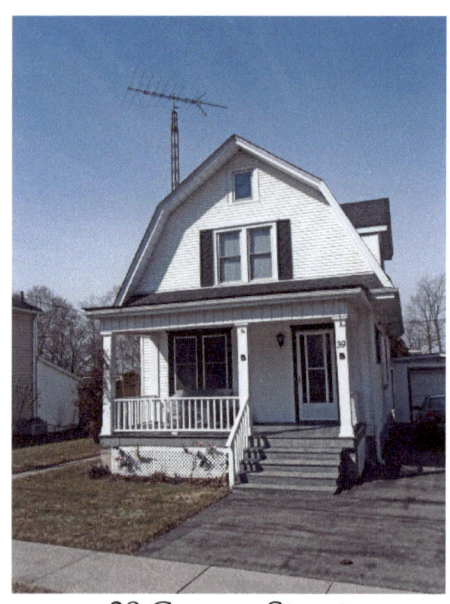
39 Cayuga Street

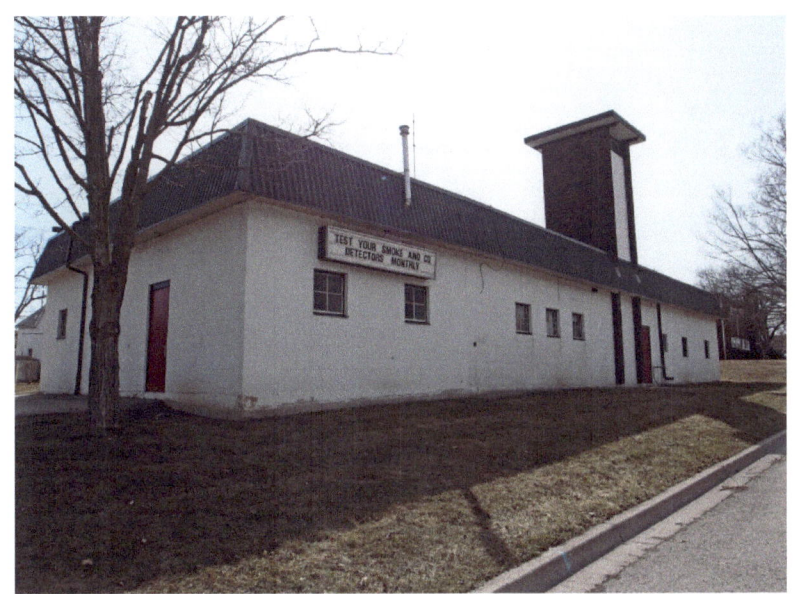

Cayuga Street – old fire hall

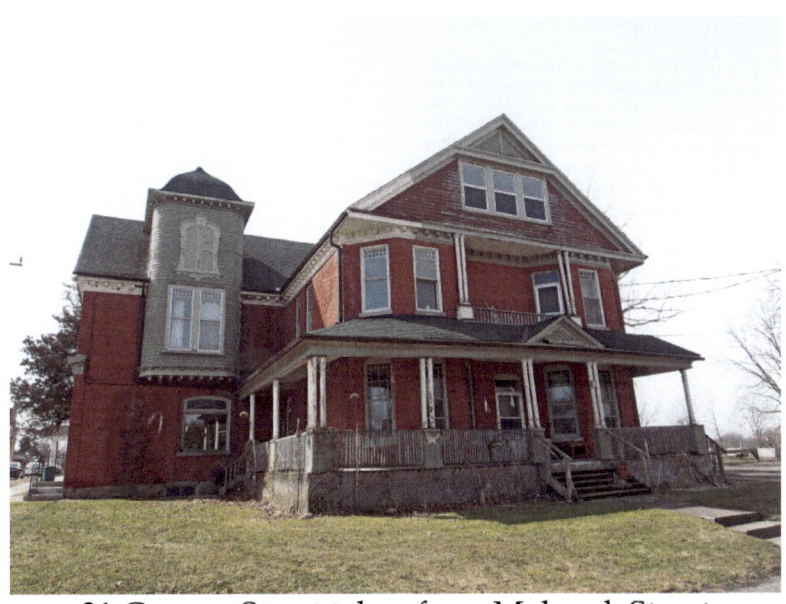

31 Cayuga Street taken from Mohawk Street

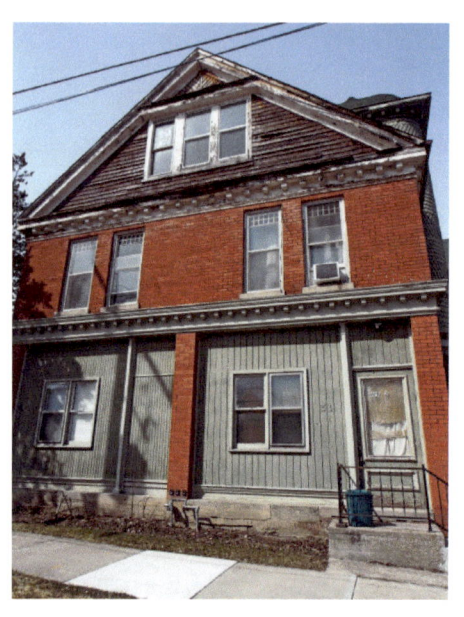

31 Cayuga Street

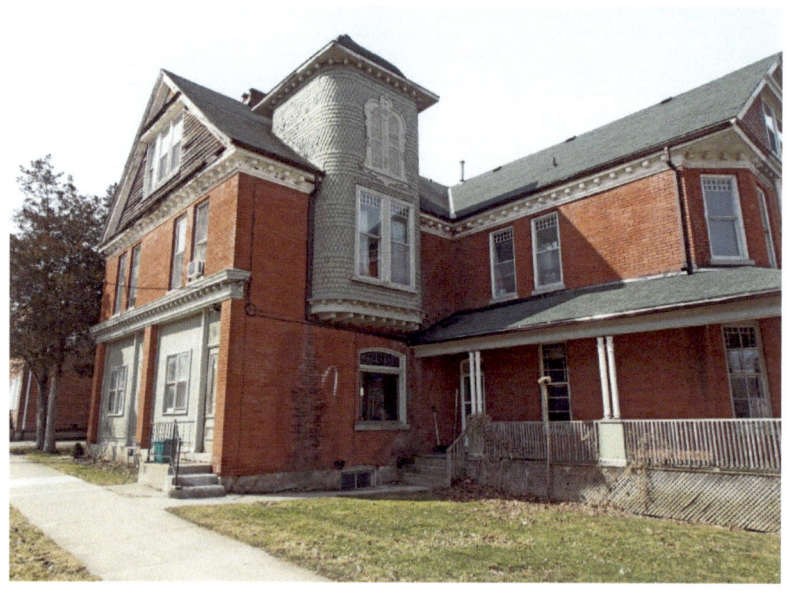

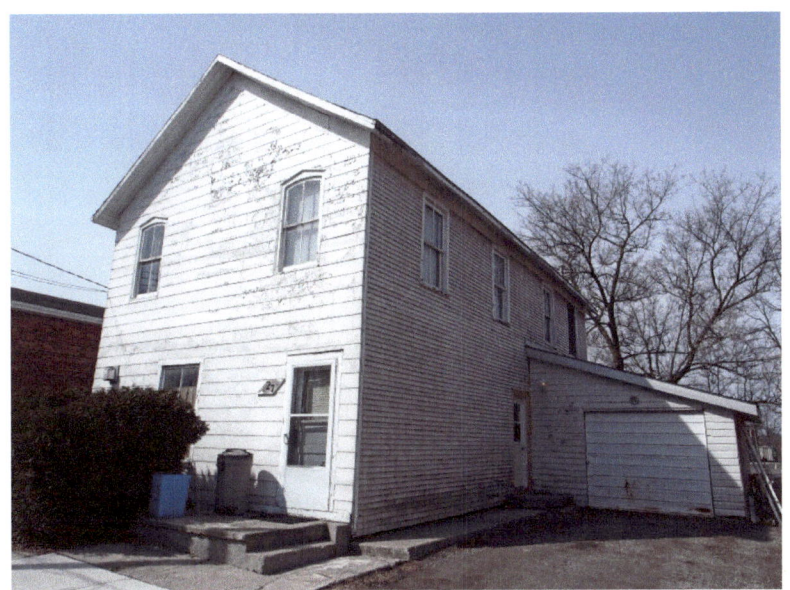

27 Cayuga Street

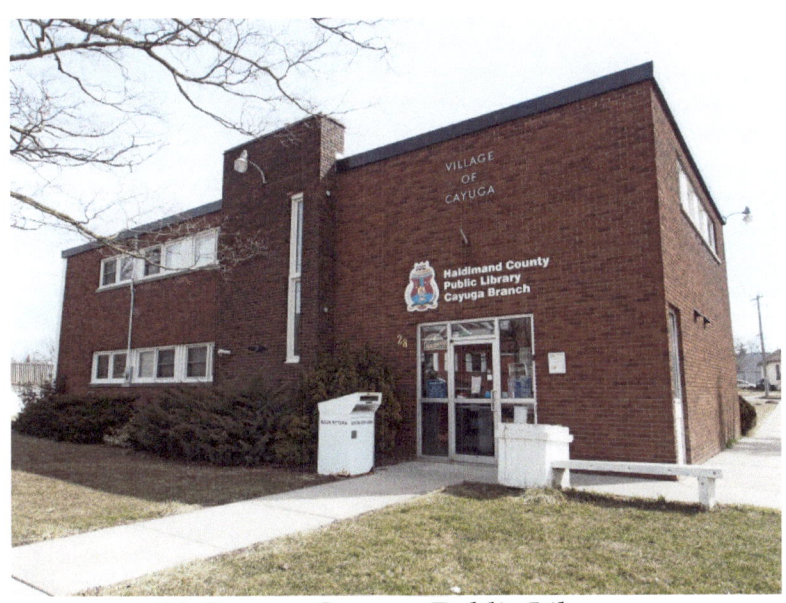

28 Cayuga Street – Public Library

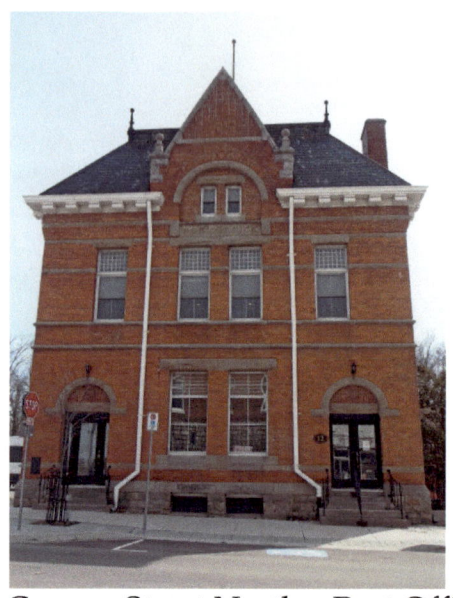

12 Cayuga Street North – Post Office

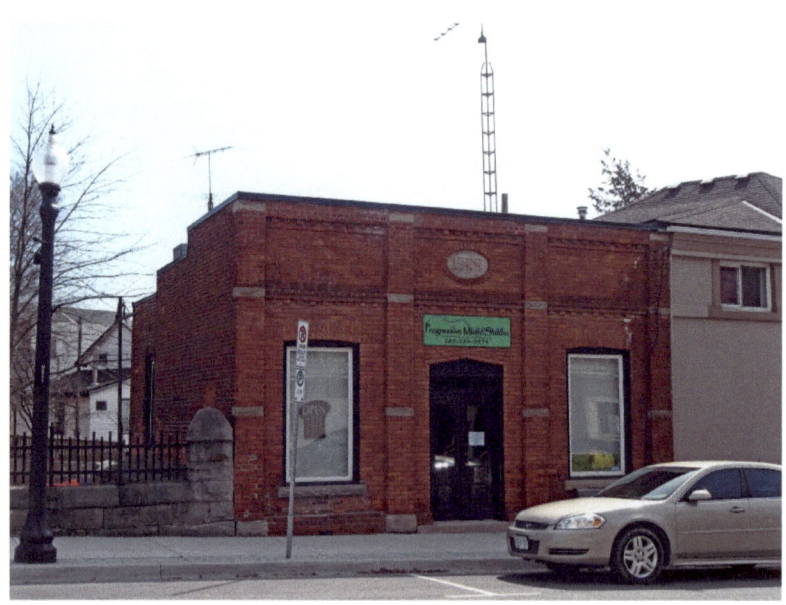

Cayuga Street North

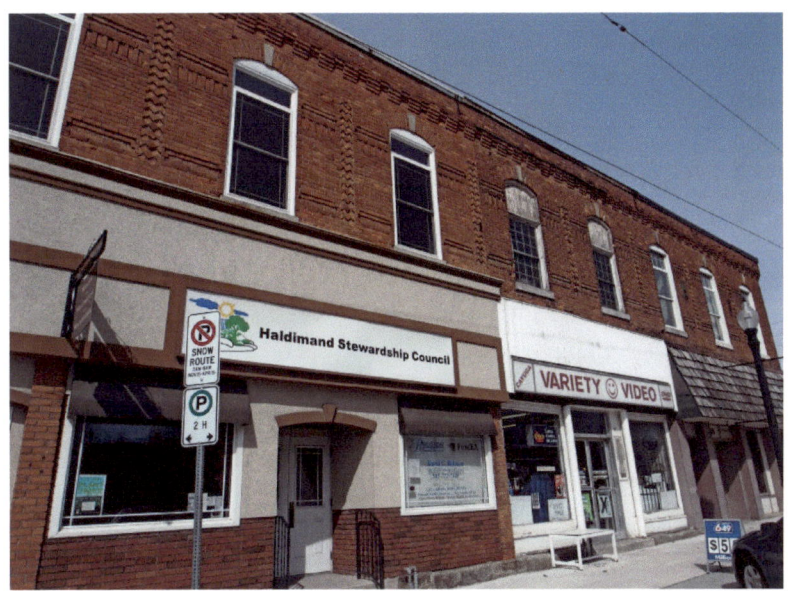

Cayuga Street North – Gibson-Bunn Building (c. 1868-1880) – inlaid diamond and rectangular brickwork on the front façade of the building, arched voussoirs with keystone above all windows

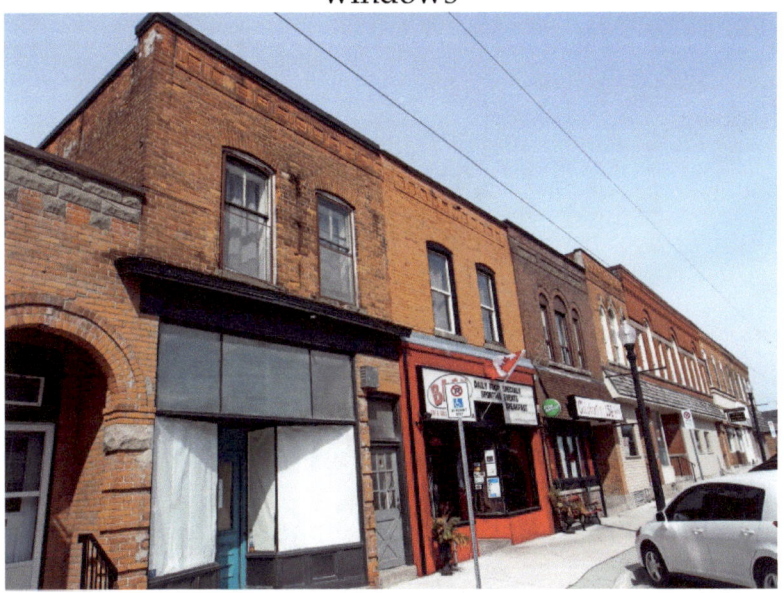

Cayuga Street North

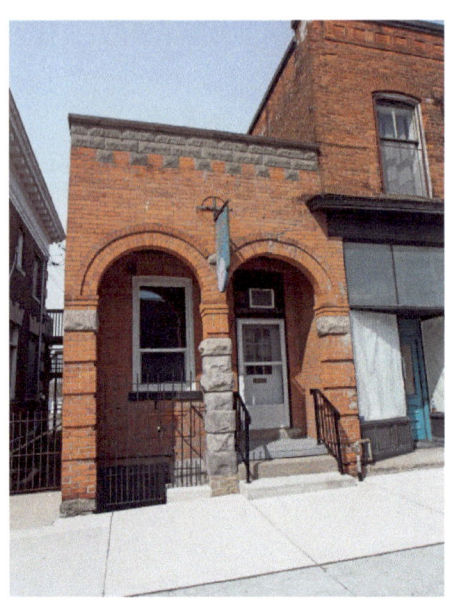

Cayuga Street North

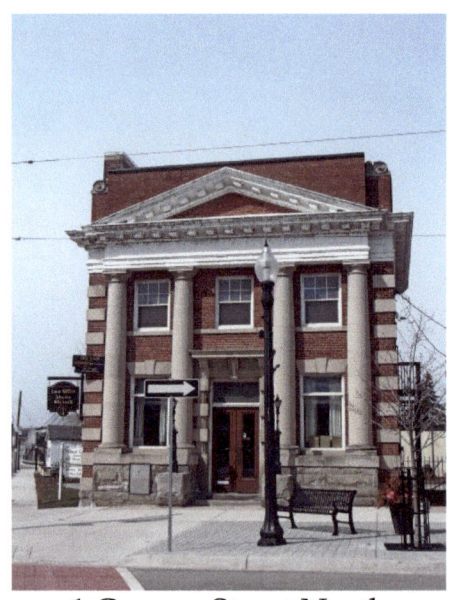

1 Cayuga Street North

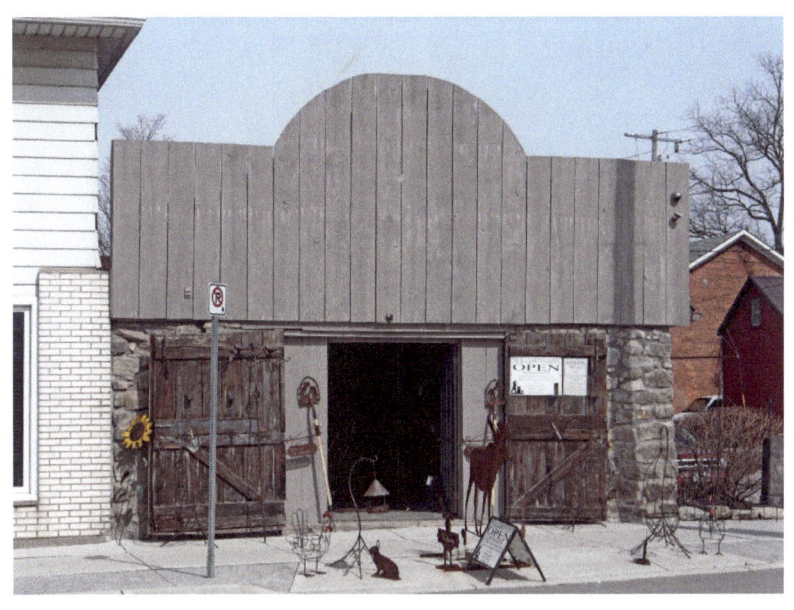

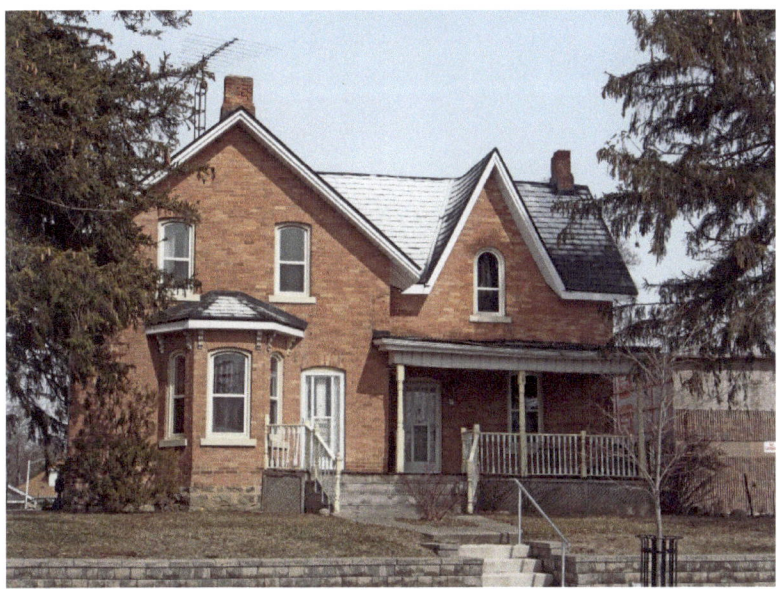

4 Talbot Street

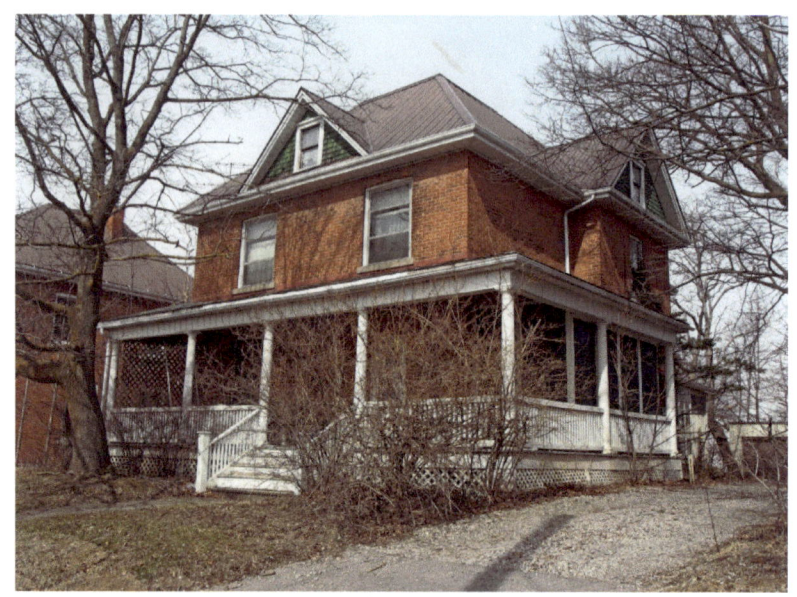
6 Talbot Street

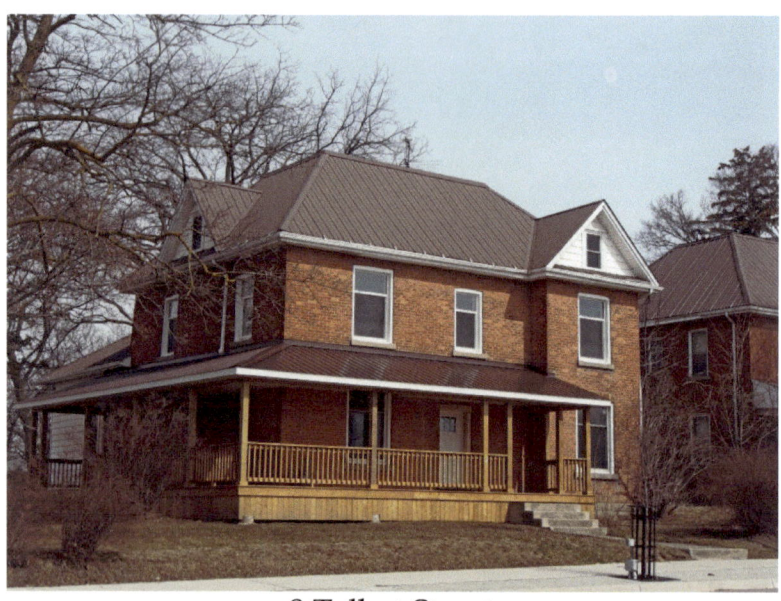
8 Talbot Street

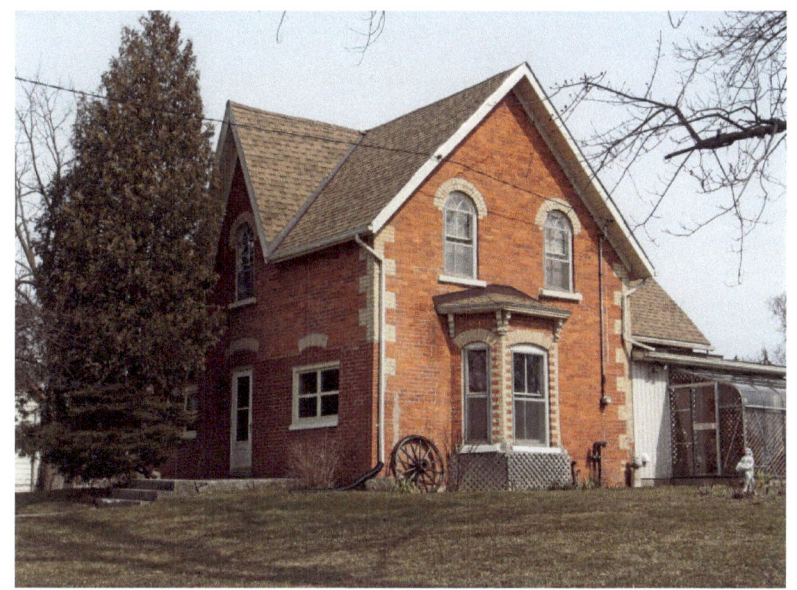

#12

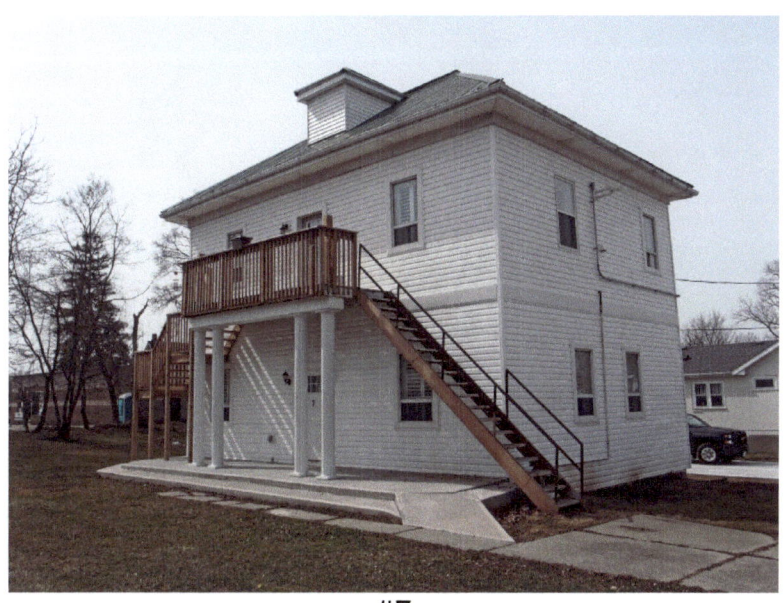

#7

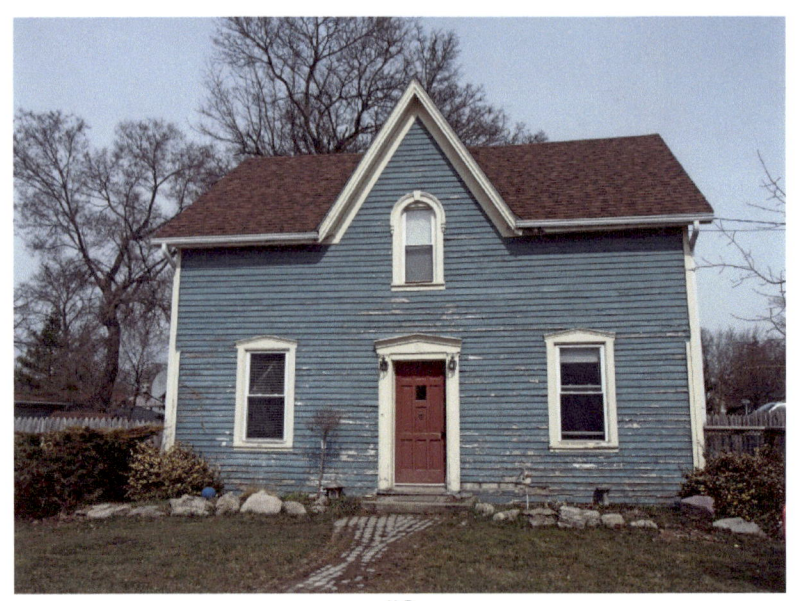
#2

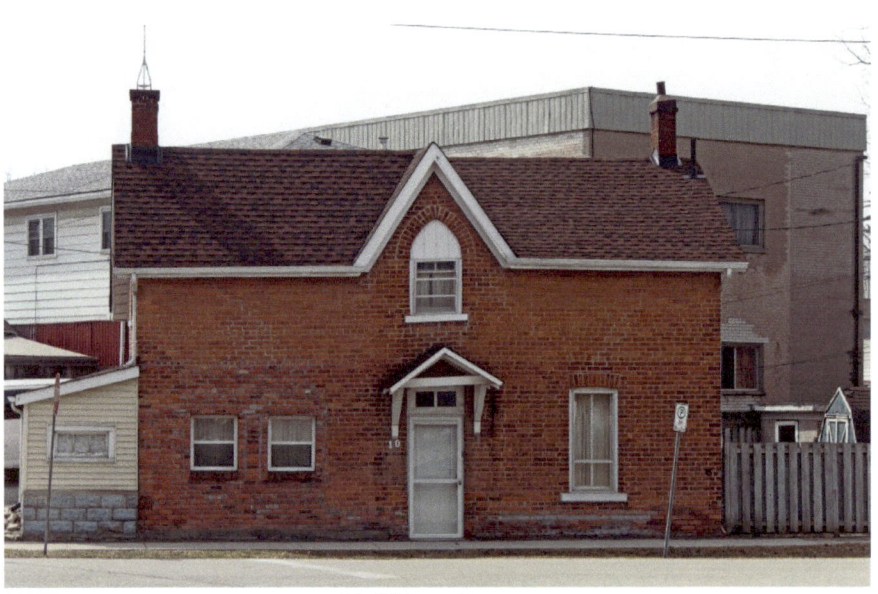
10 King Street

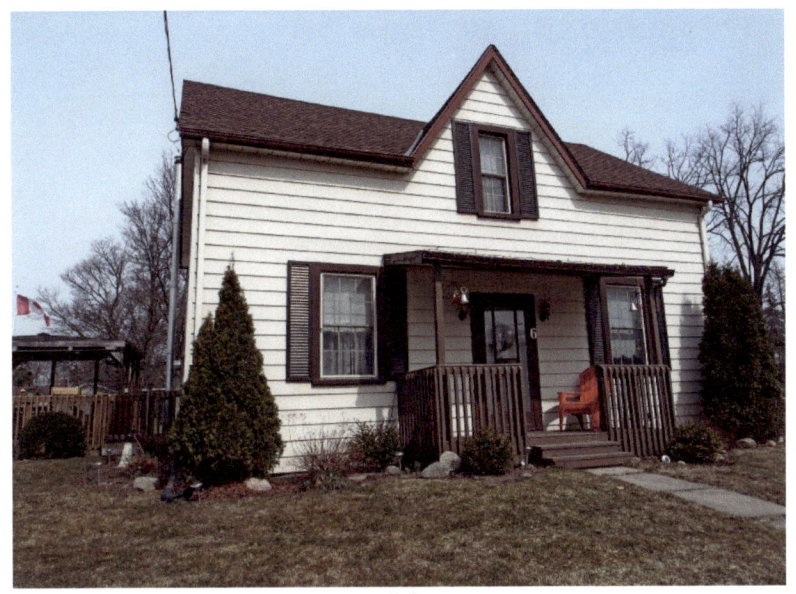

#6

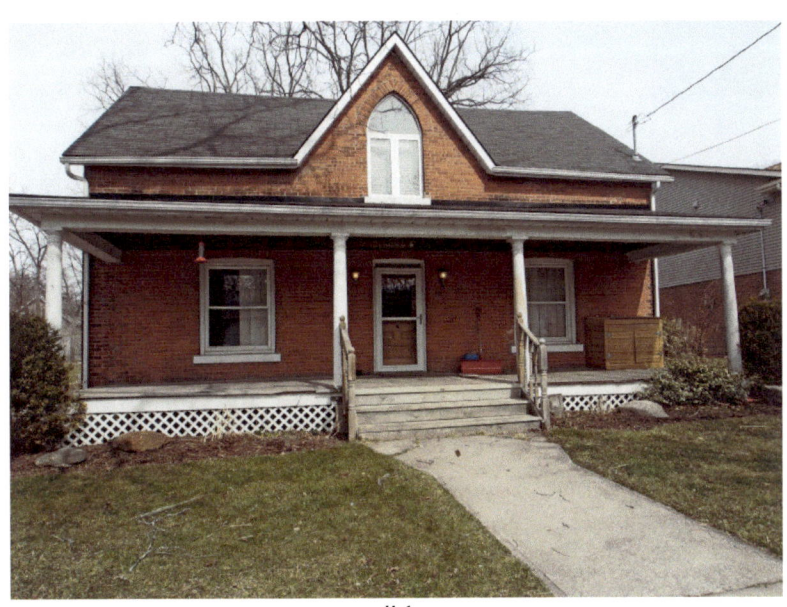

#4

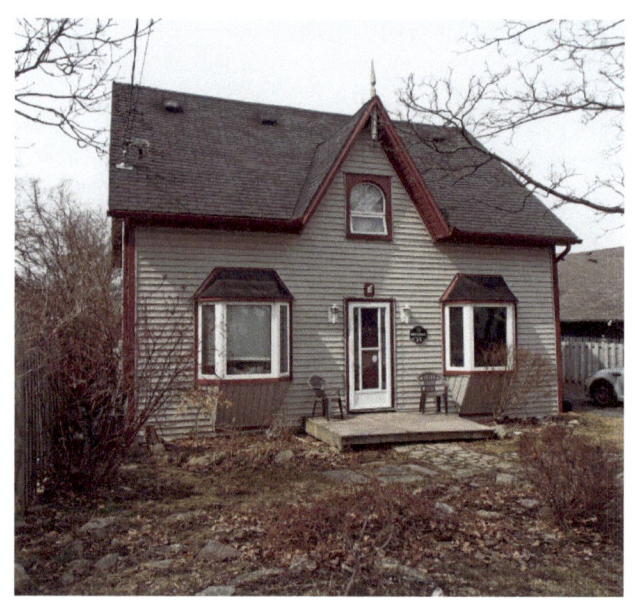

#25

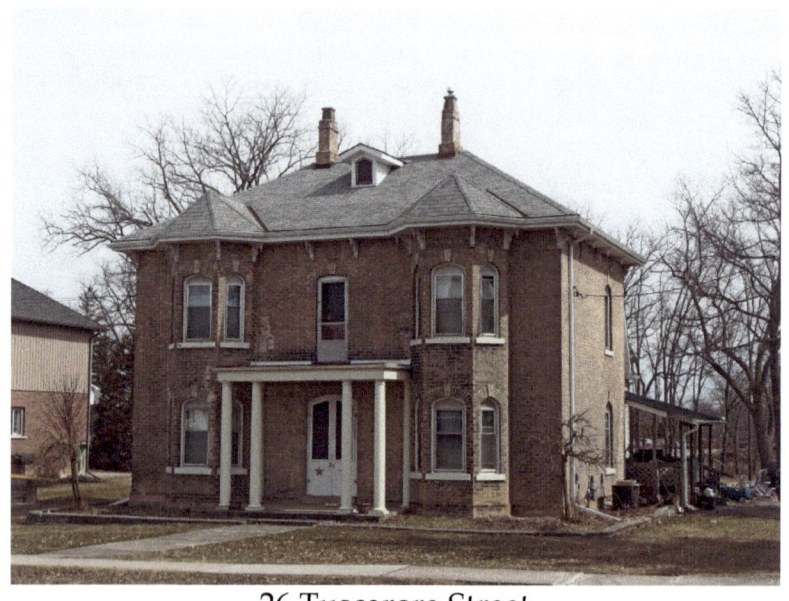

26 Tuscarora Street

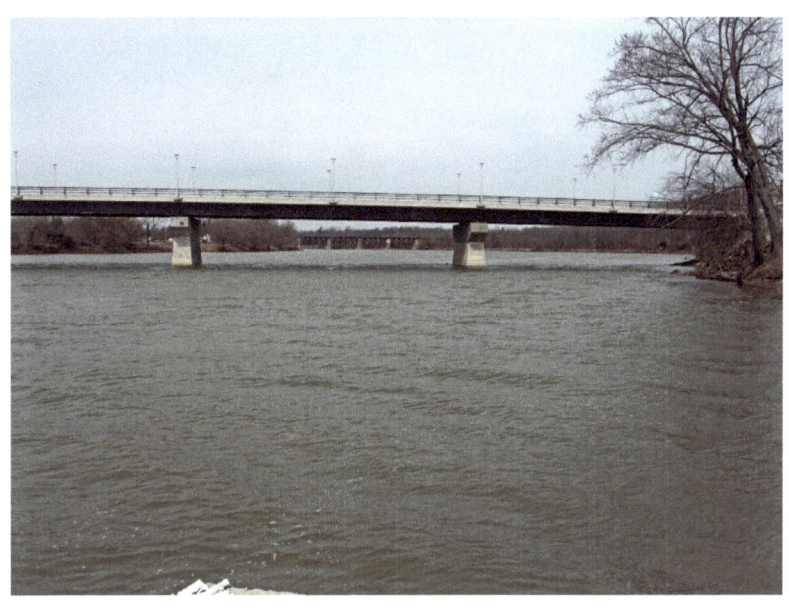

Grand River

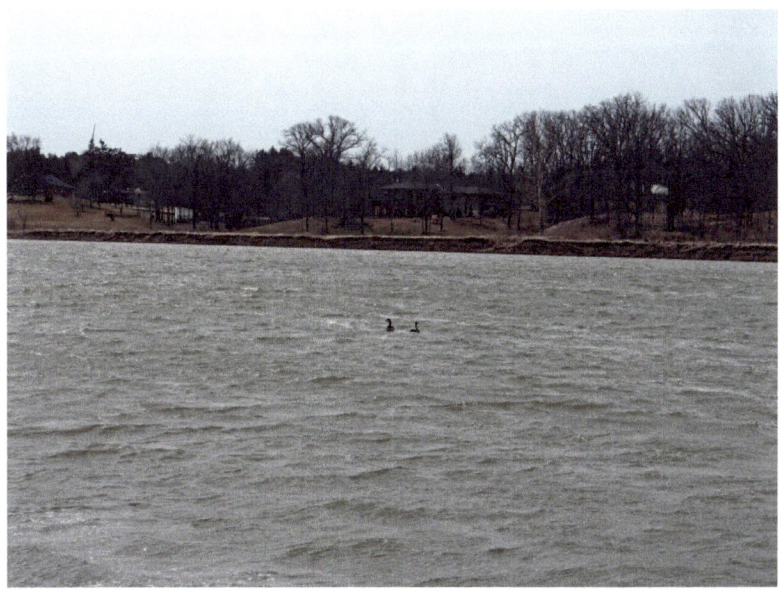

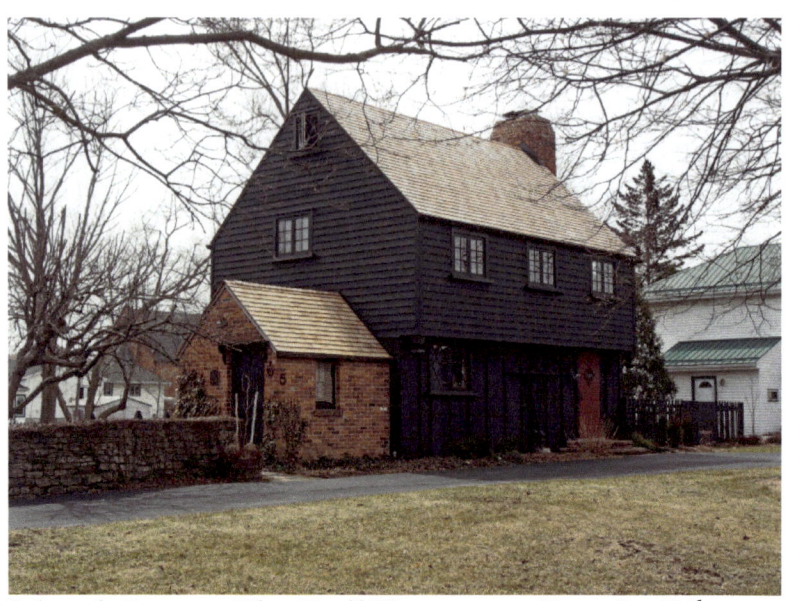

5 Mohawk Street – The Duff House - replica of a 17th century New England Garrison style house – steep pitched cedar-shake A-roof, second story overhang, double casement wooden windows

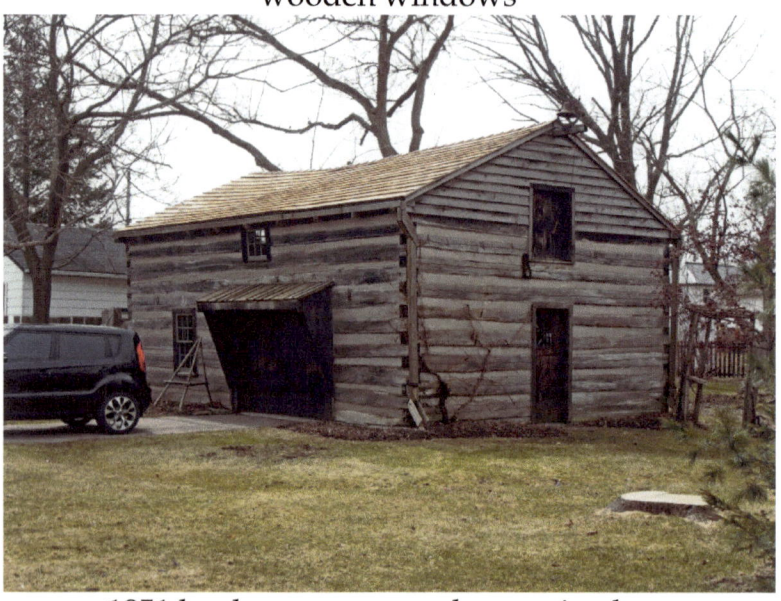

1851 log house – square hewn pine logs

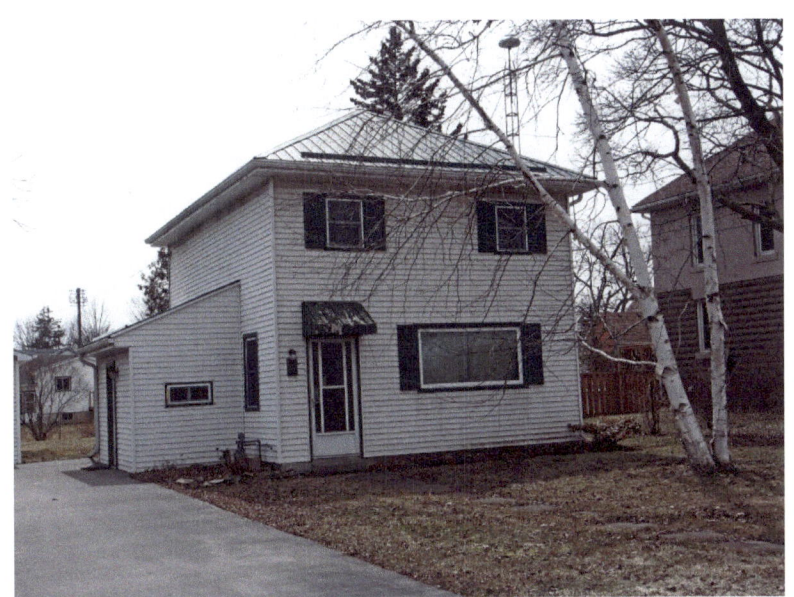

3 Mohawk Street

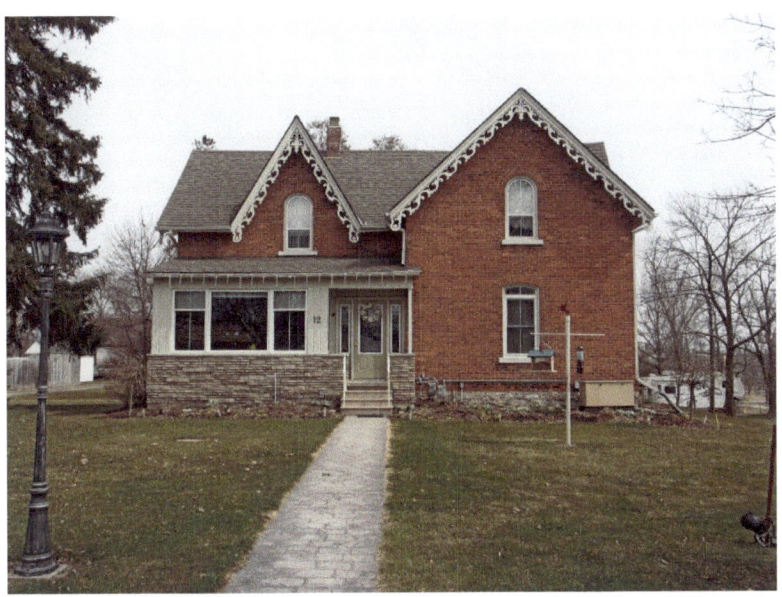

12 Winnett Street – Ye Olde Rectory – c. 1880

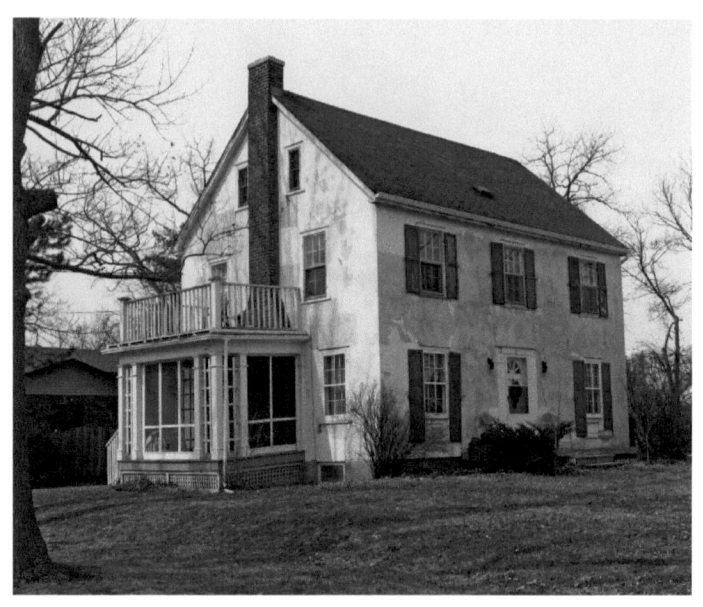

17 Winnett Street

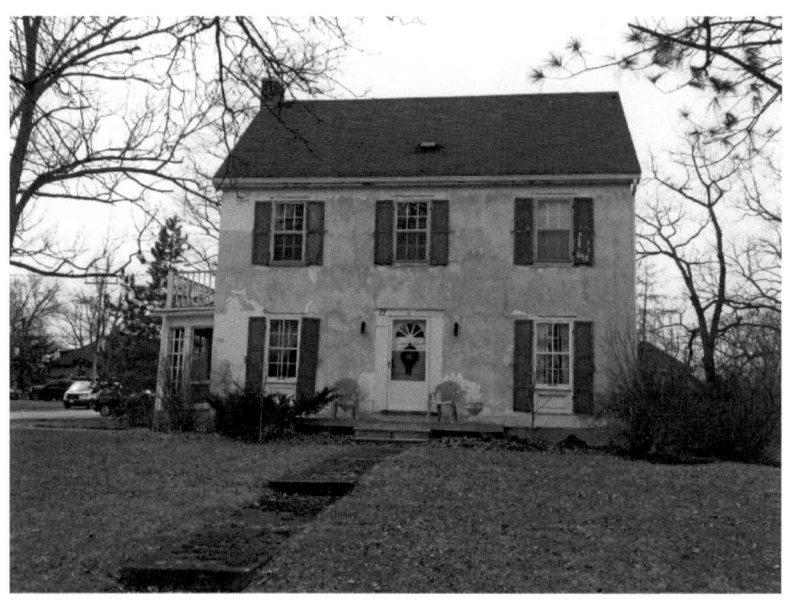

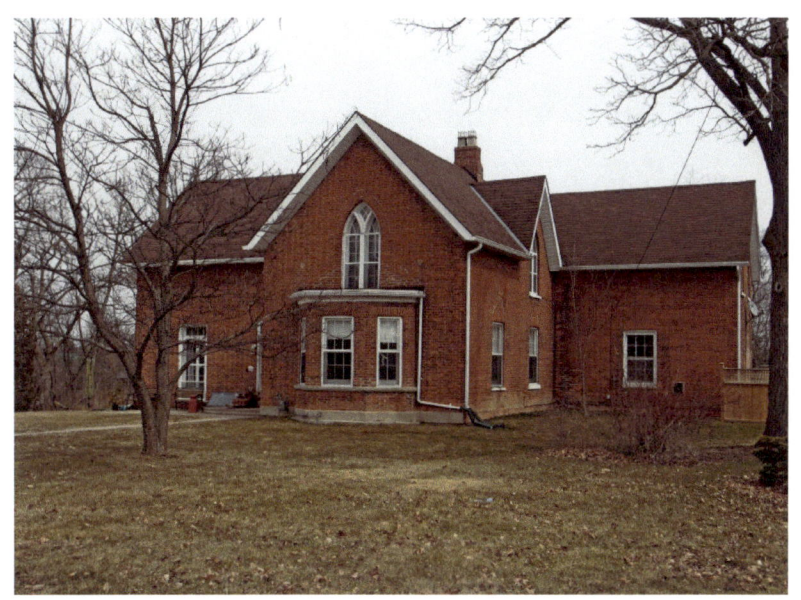

24 Winnett Street

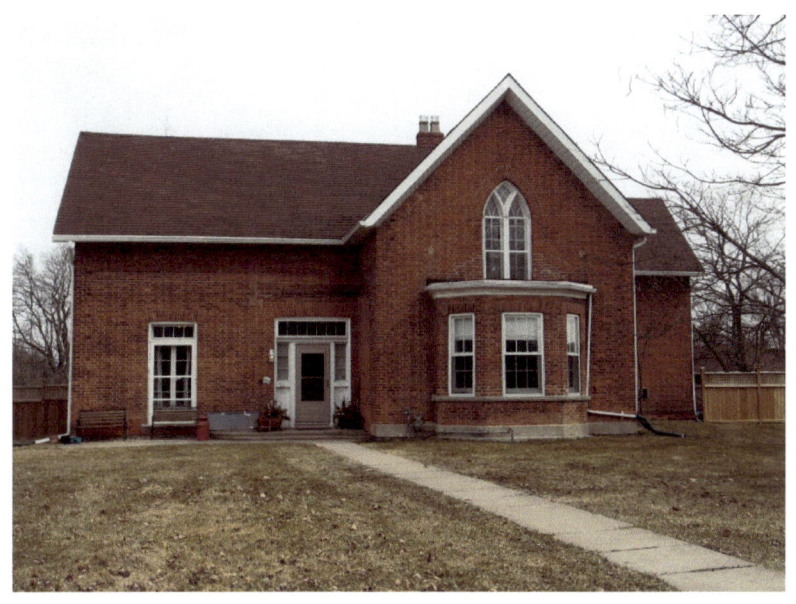

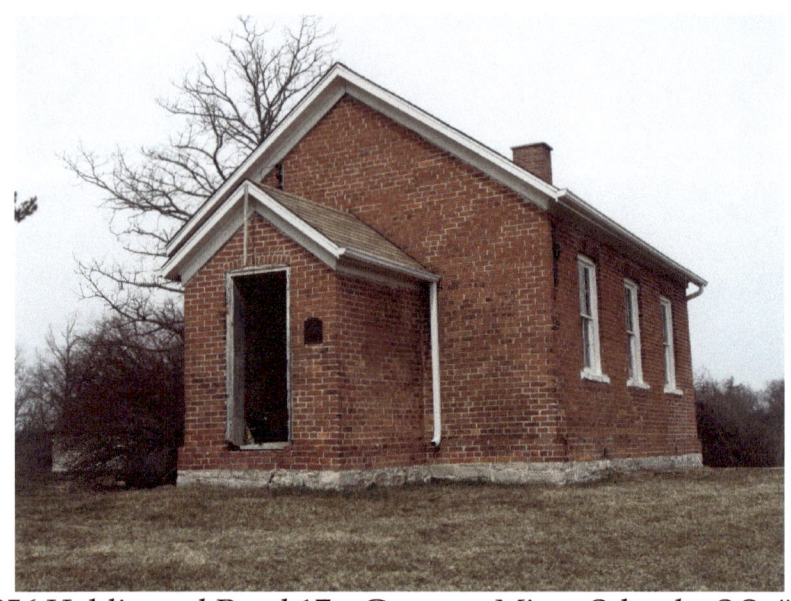

1956 Haldimand Road 17 – Gypsum Mines School – S.S. #10
North Cayuga – c. 1874

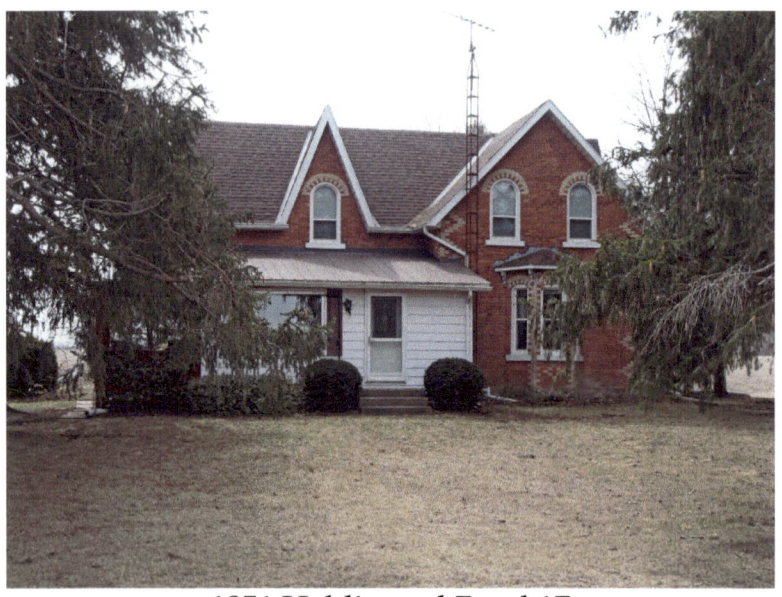

1951 Haldimand Road 17

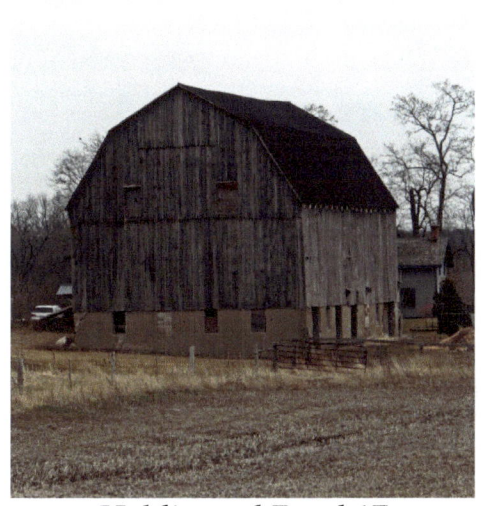

Haldimand Road 17

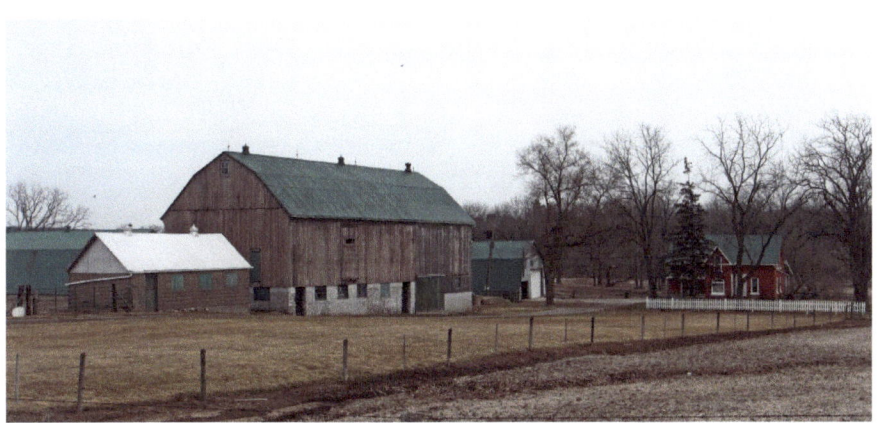

Haldimand Road 17

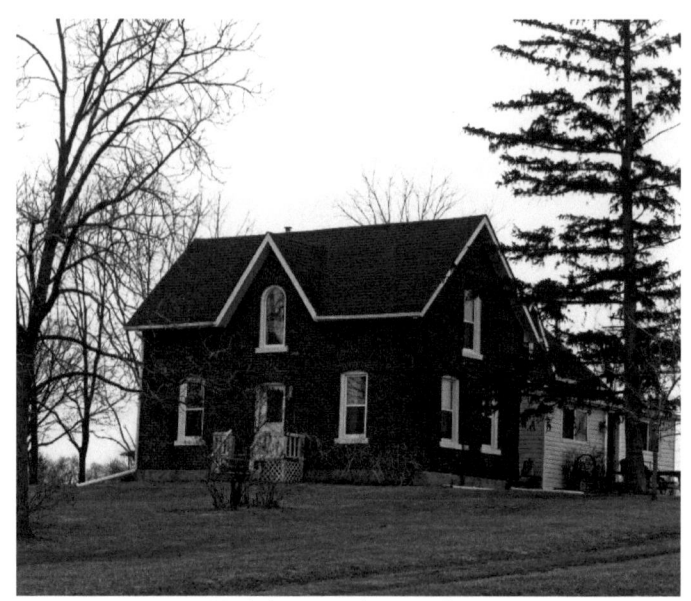
Haldimand Road 17

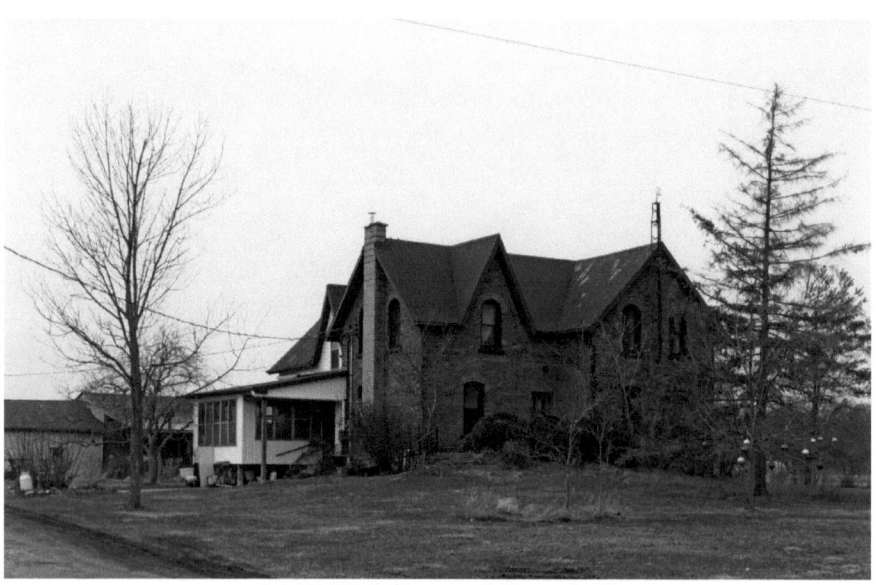
1465 Haldimand Road 17

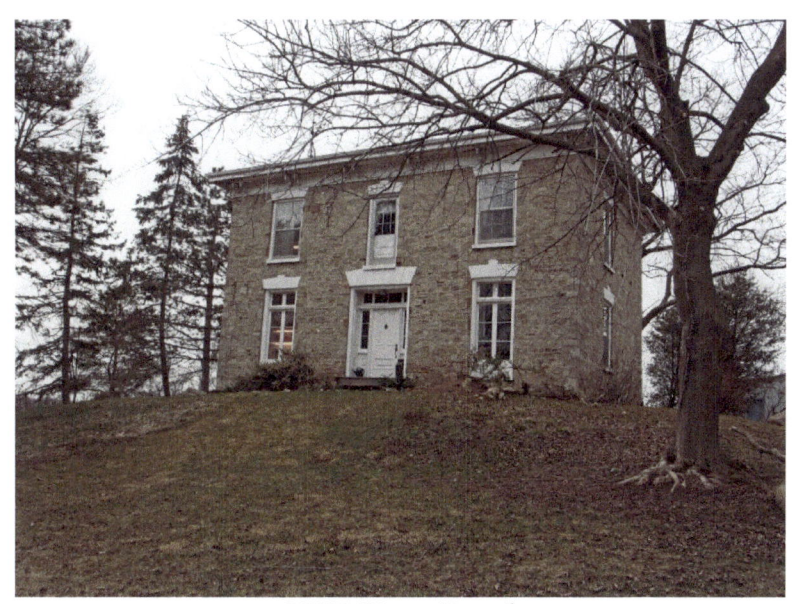

2935 River Road

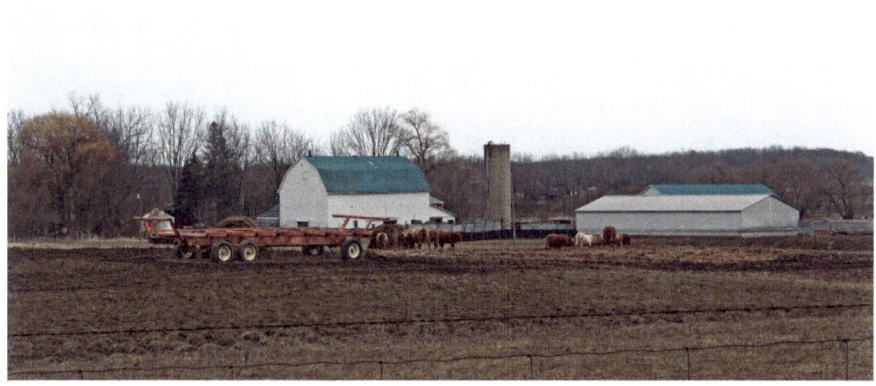

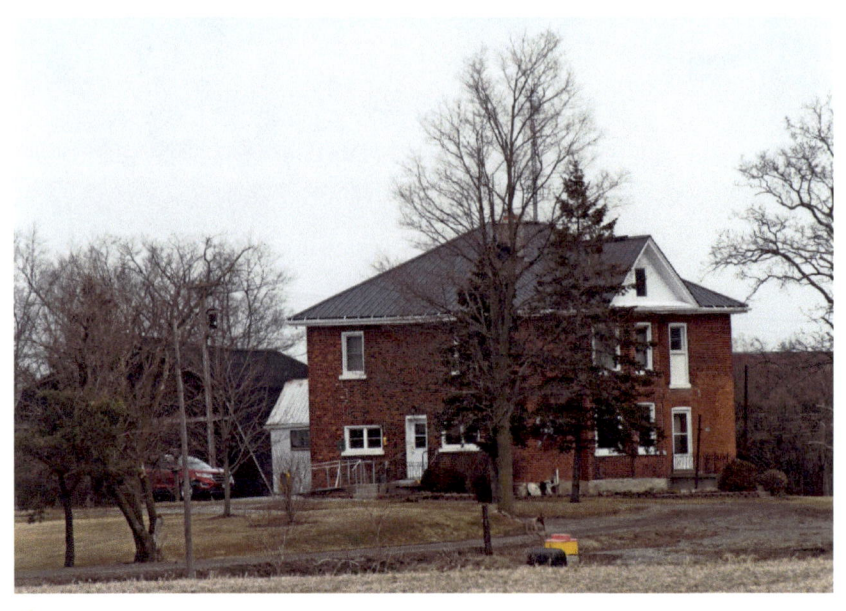

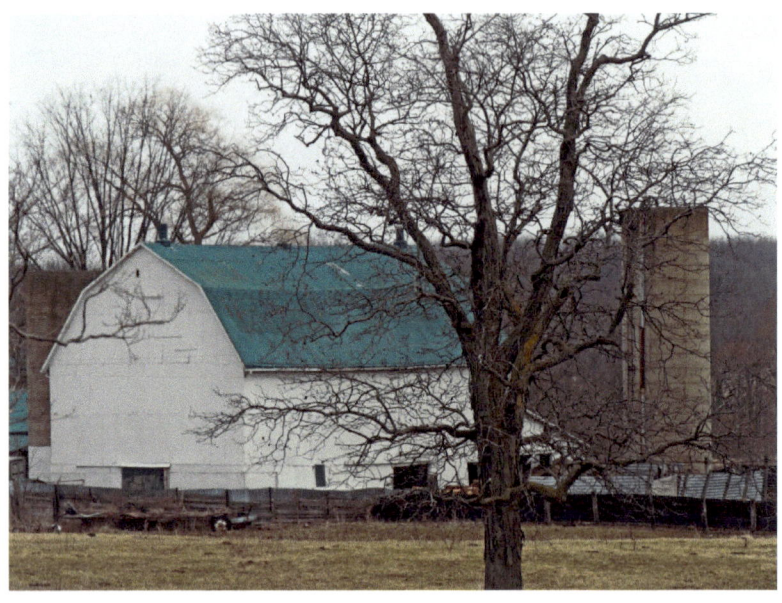

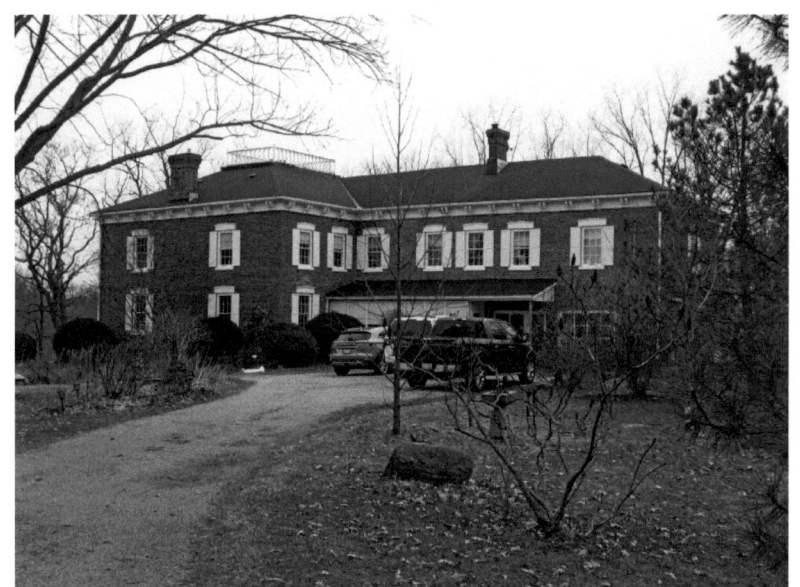

3220 River Road – Dochstader Hotel (Olson House) was built in 1853 in the early and active settlement of Mount Healy, once the center of social activity in the area.

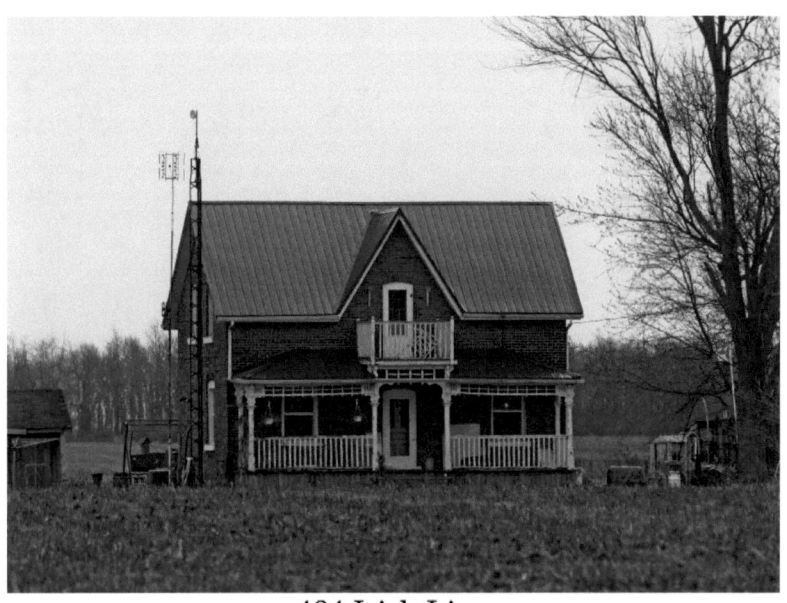

404 Irish Line

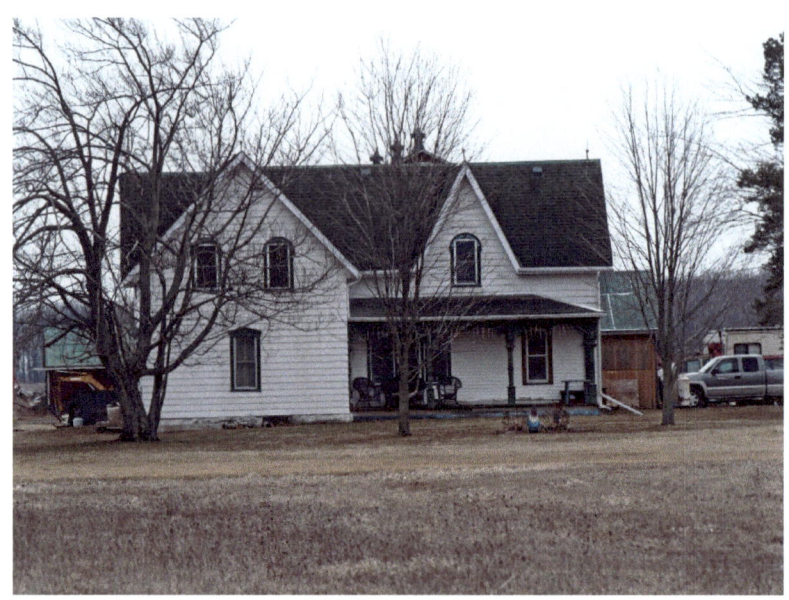

360 Irish Line

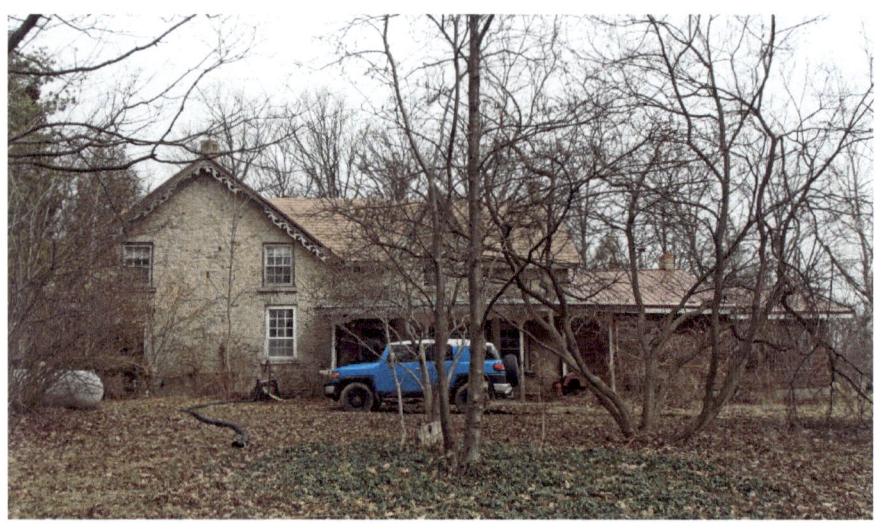

266 Irish Line – stone masonry dating from 1850s, and other masonry from the 1890s; verge board trim on gables

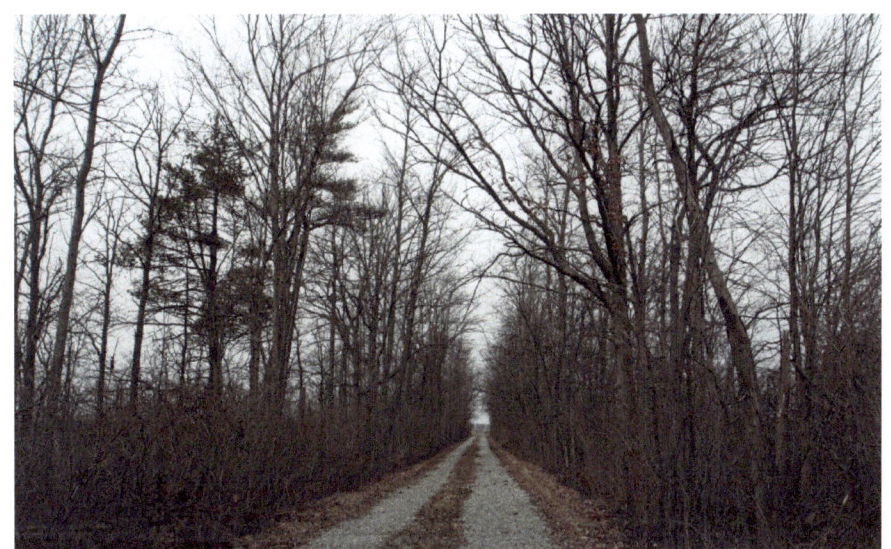

Irish Line

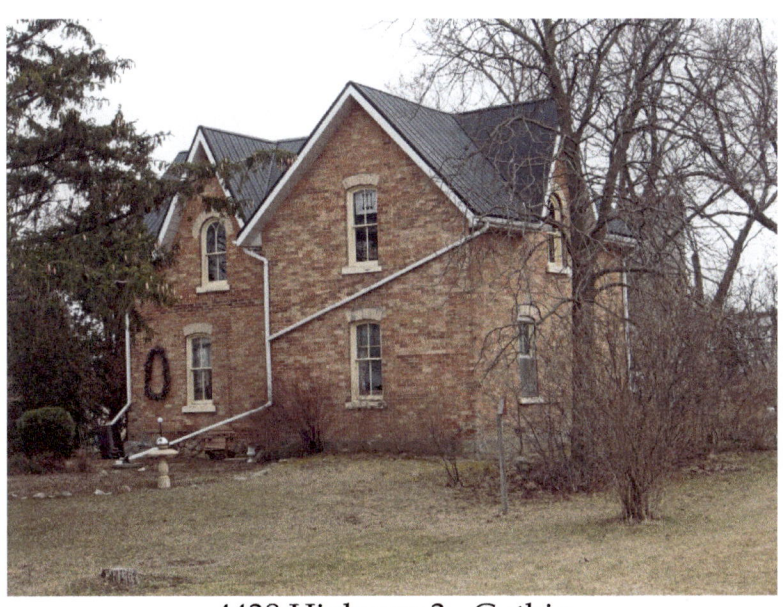

4438 Highway 3 - Gothic

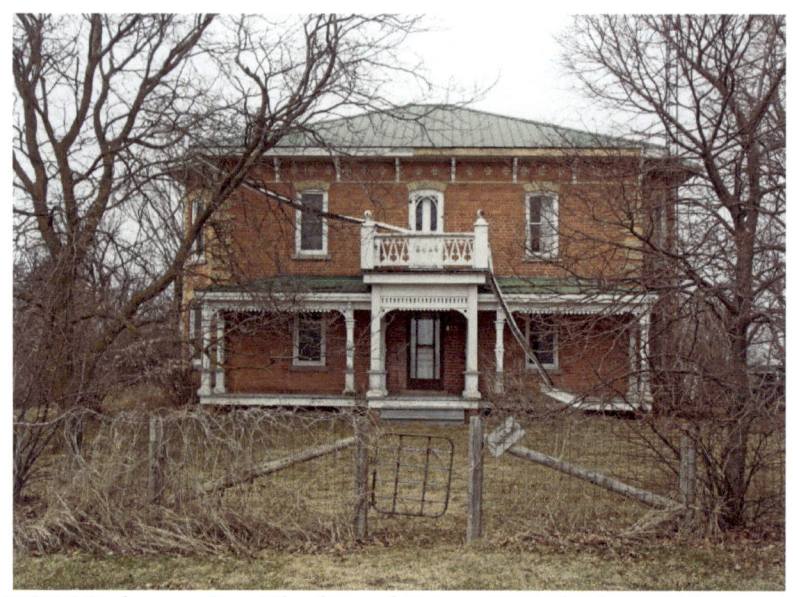

4135 Highway 3 – Clark and Mary Vanderburgh house – patterned brick Italianate farmhouse – 1890 – cornice brackets, second floor balcony, full width veranda

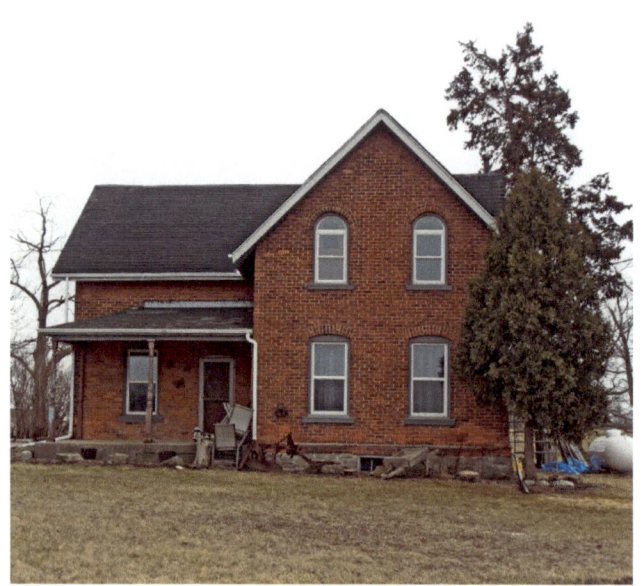

4384 Highway 3

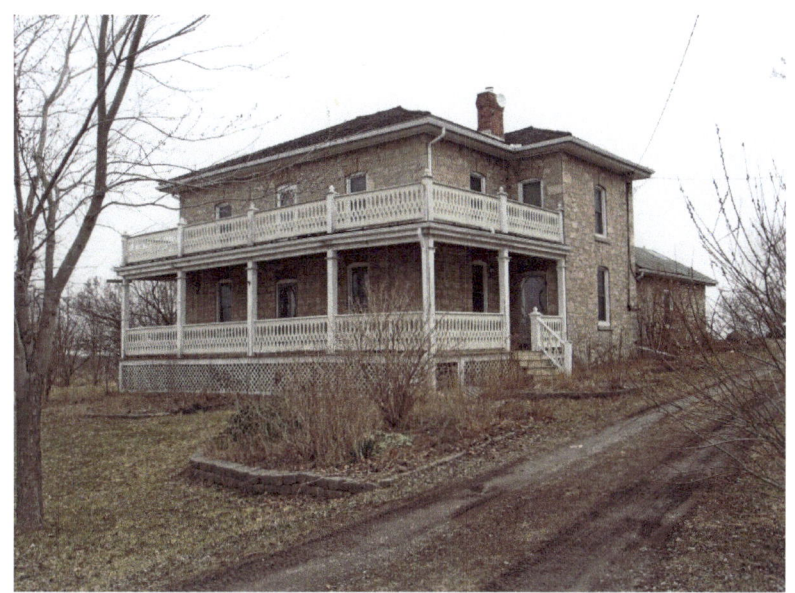

4104 Highway 3 – Campbell-Pine House – c. 1895 – limestone farmhouse with hipped roof, two-story veranda; a large portion of Donald Campbell's 1847 stone cottage is incorporated into the walls of the house. Donald Campbell was one of the earliest settlers of North Cayuga Township; he operated a steam sawmill on the premises.

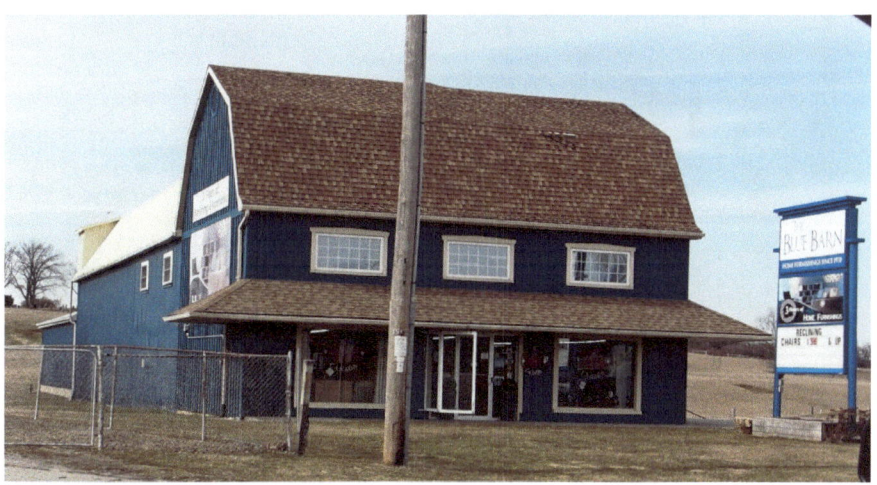

4929 Highway 3 - The Blue Barn – furniture store

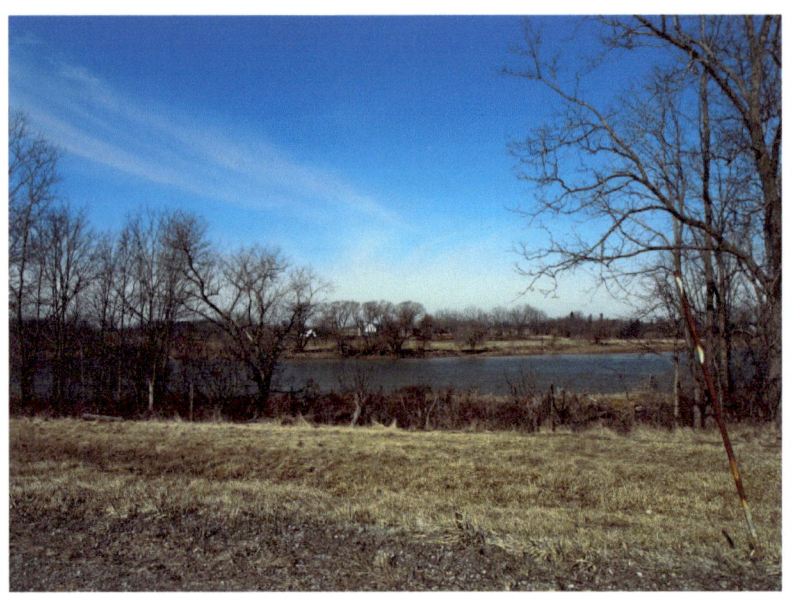

This land beside the Grand River was part of the tract granted to Adam Young and his family for their loyalty to the Crown during the American Revolution. The Youngs are remembered as one of the families who helped to build the new and growing country of Canada.

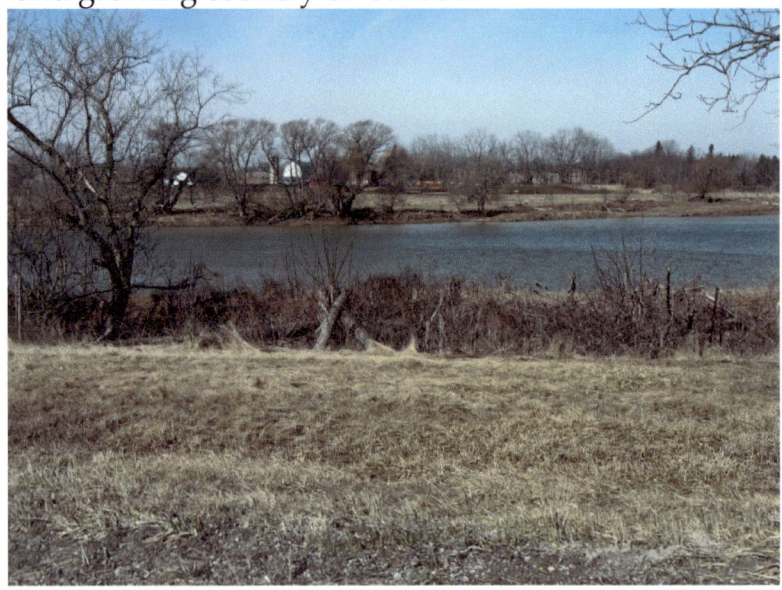

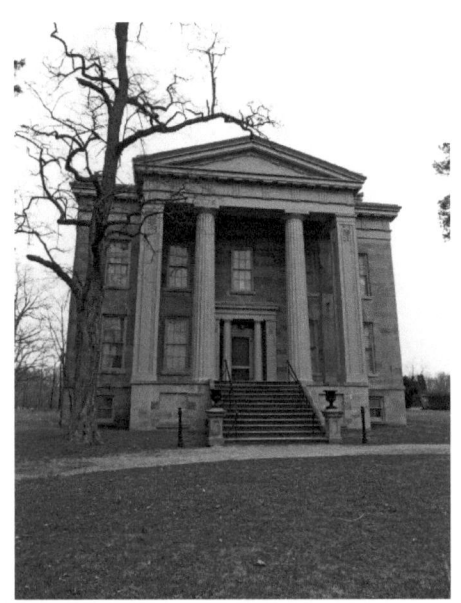

243 Haldimand Highway 54 - Ruthven Estate, the main house and wing, c. 1845, was designed by the master building/ architect John Latshaw. Ruthven Park is a 1,500-acre country estate. The house is in the Greek Revival style with a broad staircase leading to a front landing with classical columns. The south wing was added c. 1860, the south-east wing c. 1880, and the east wing c. 1884. It was the former home of five generations of the Thompson family from the 1840s to 1990s.

David Thompson came to the area and started a saw mill in 1834, and added a grist mill in 1836. David was instrumental in the laying out of the former 1200 acre town of Indiana. He eventually owned two sawmills, as well as a gristmill, carding mill, cooperage, and several stores. Overall, Indiana supported over thirty industries and was the largest industrial town in Haldimand County in the mid-nineteenth century.

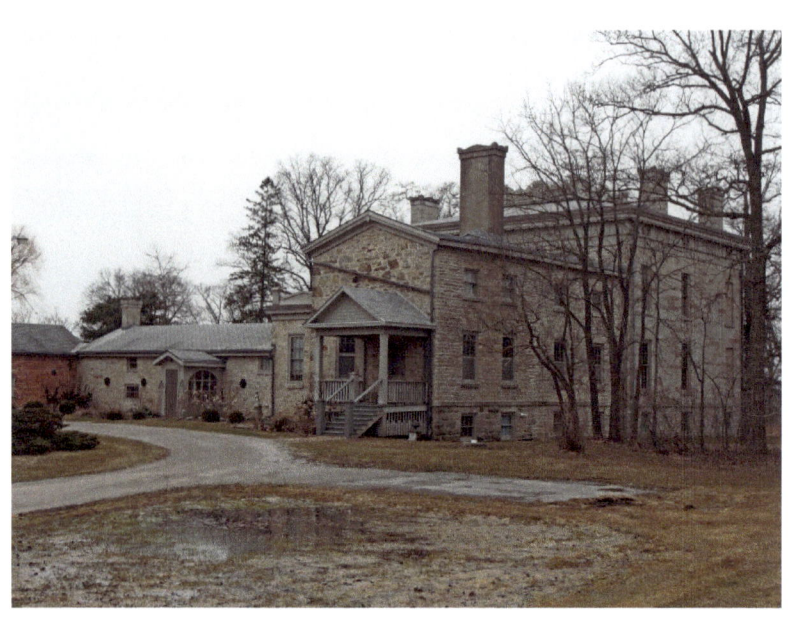

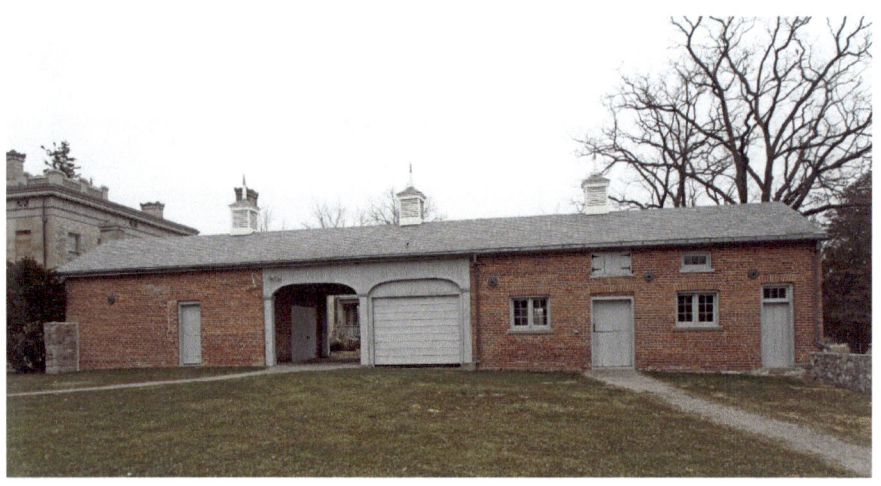

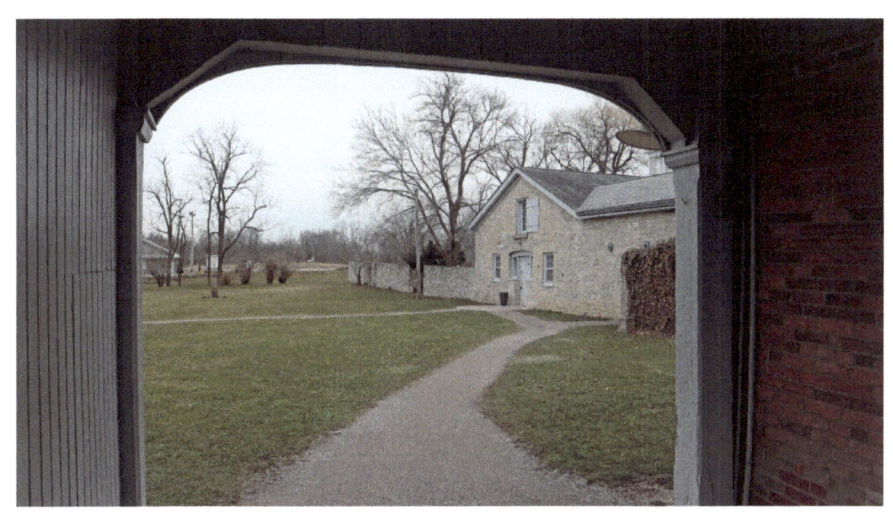

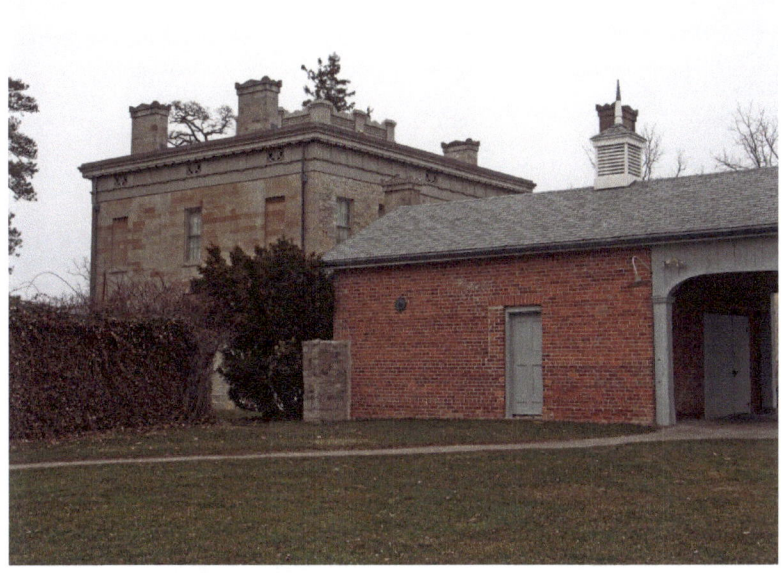

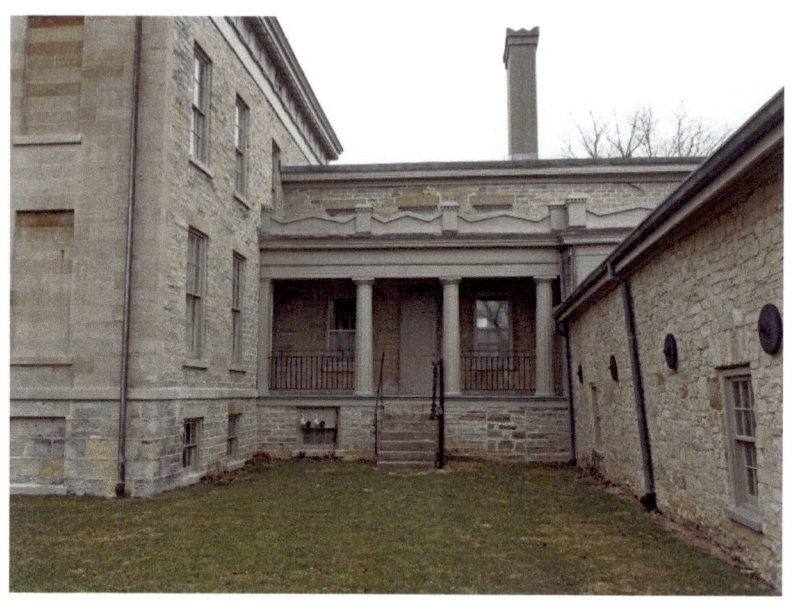

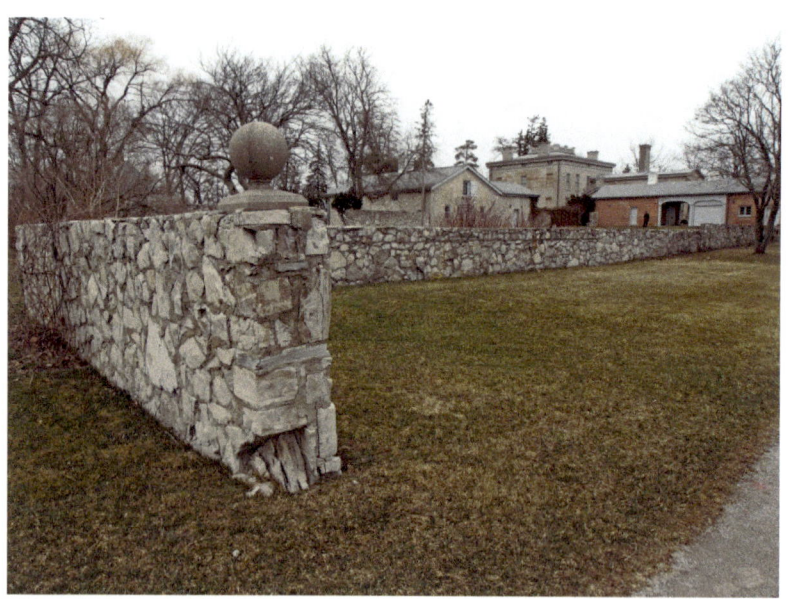

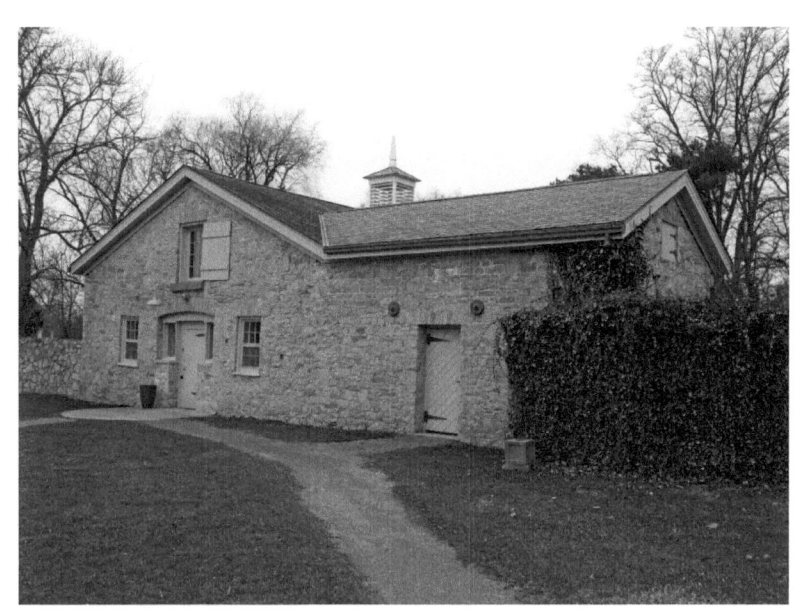

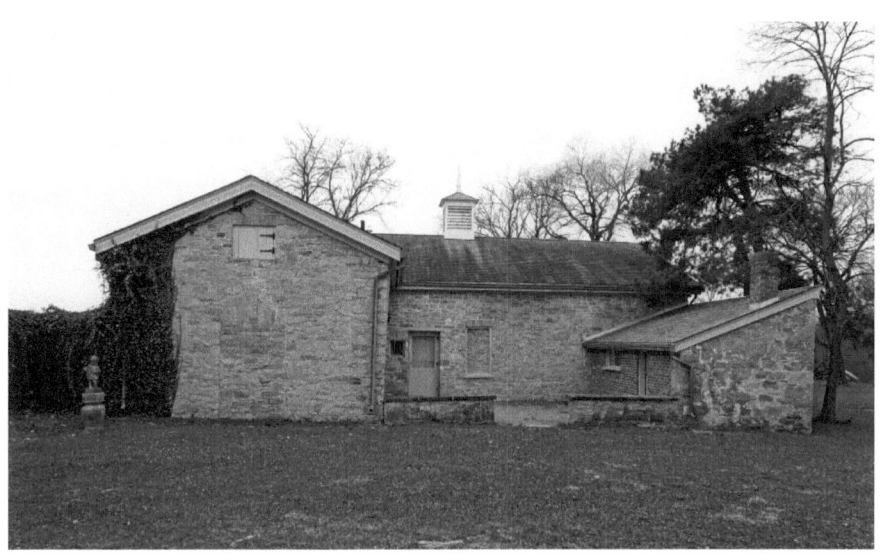

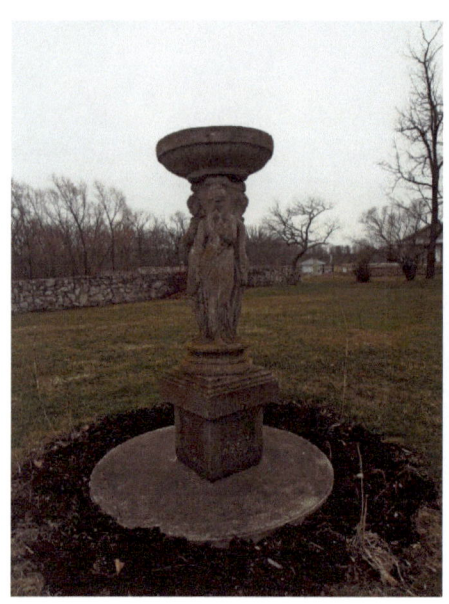 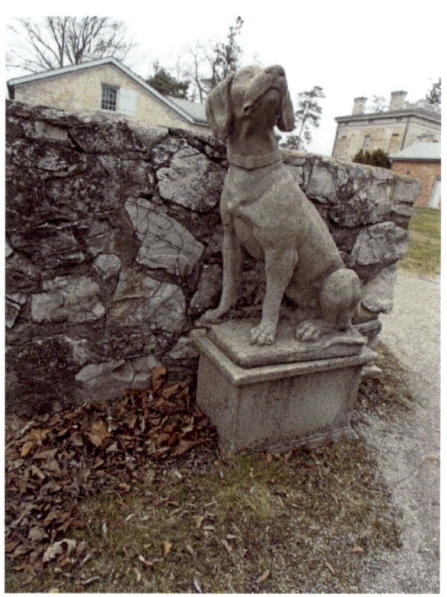 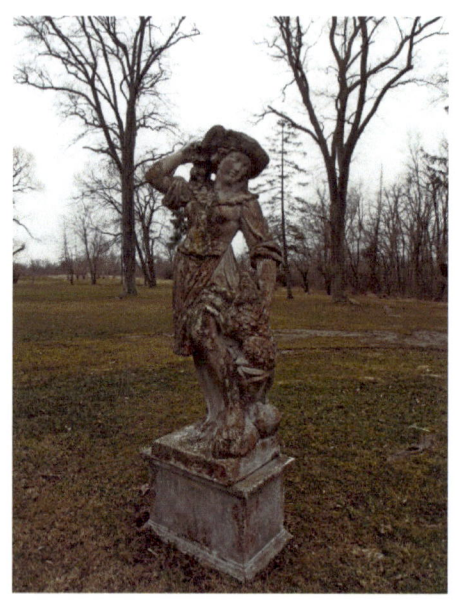

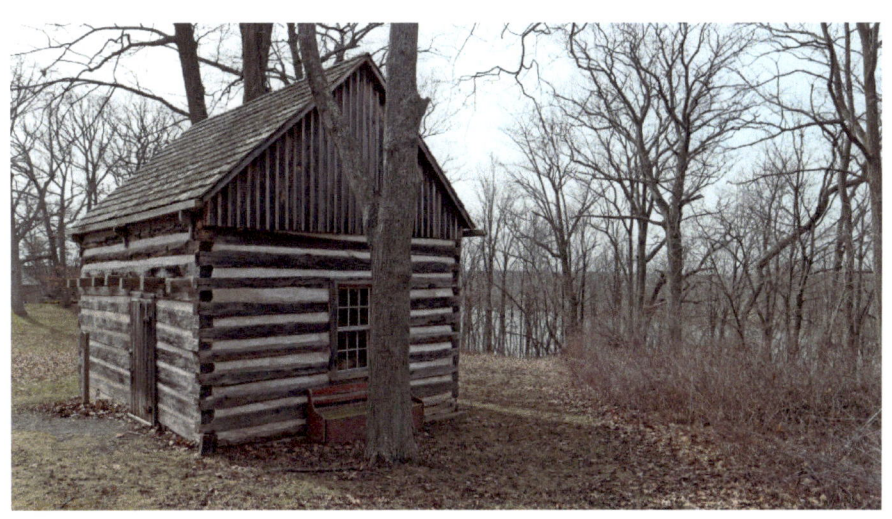

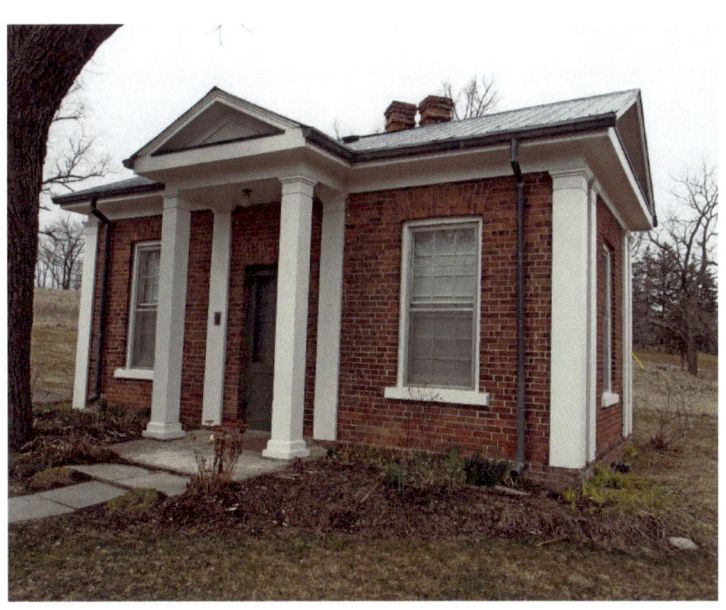

York

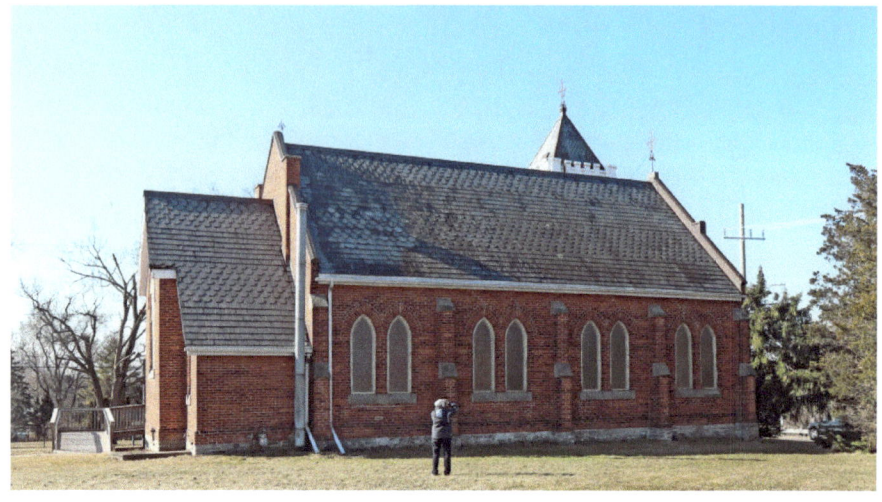

Front Street – St. John's Anglican Church

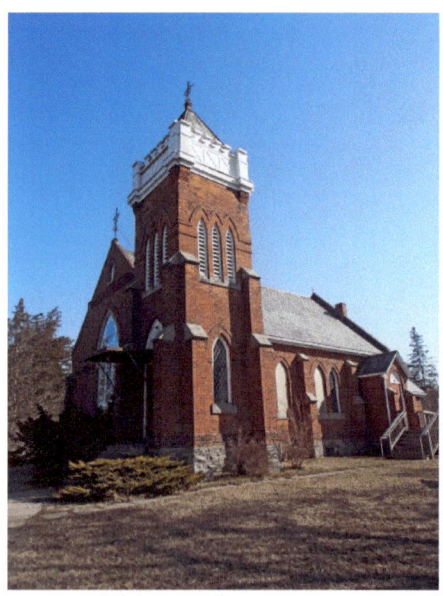
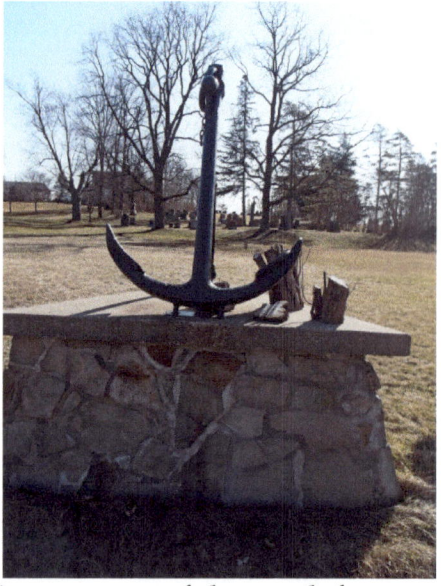

    This anchor was erected in memory of the work force involved in the construction of the canal system and the captain and crews who operated from the Port of York during the period of navigation on the Grand River after 1832.

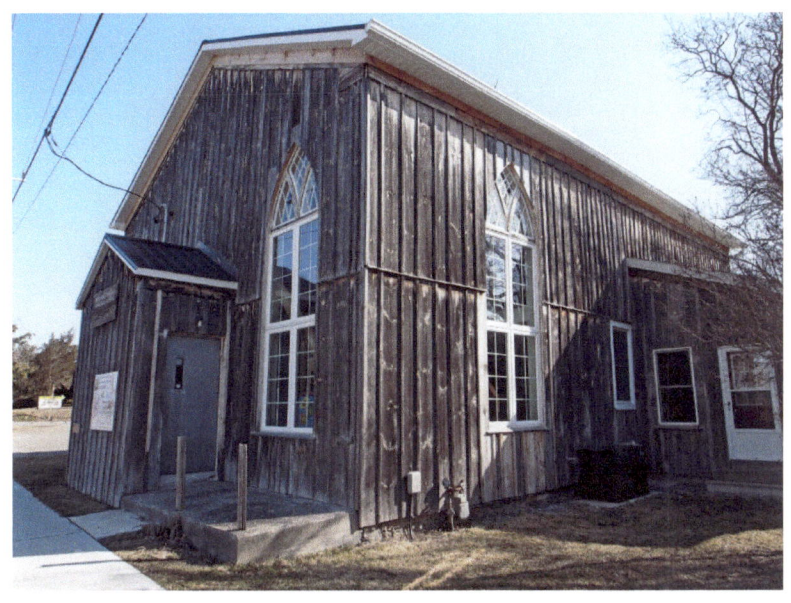

3 Front Street – St. John's Parish Hall was built about 1845-46

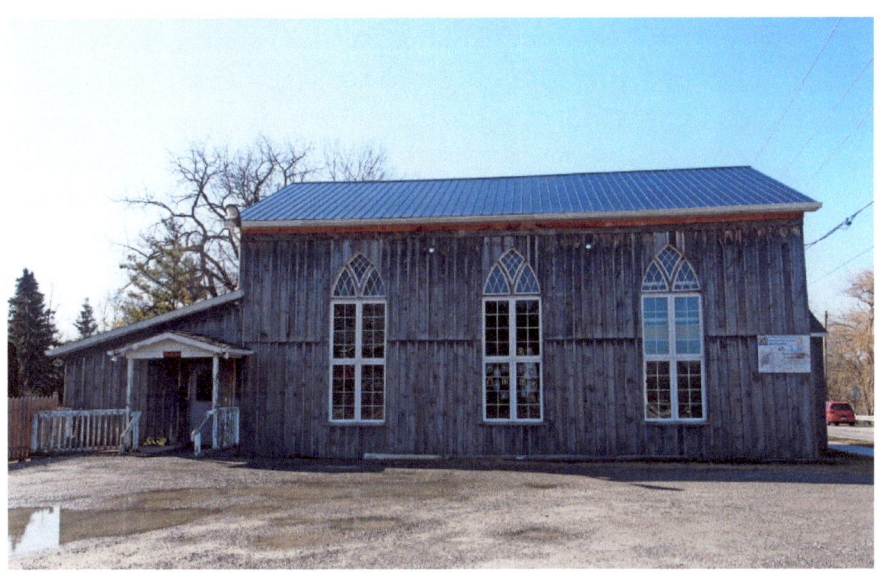

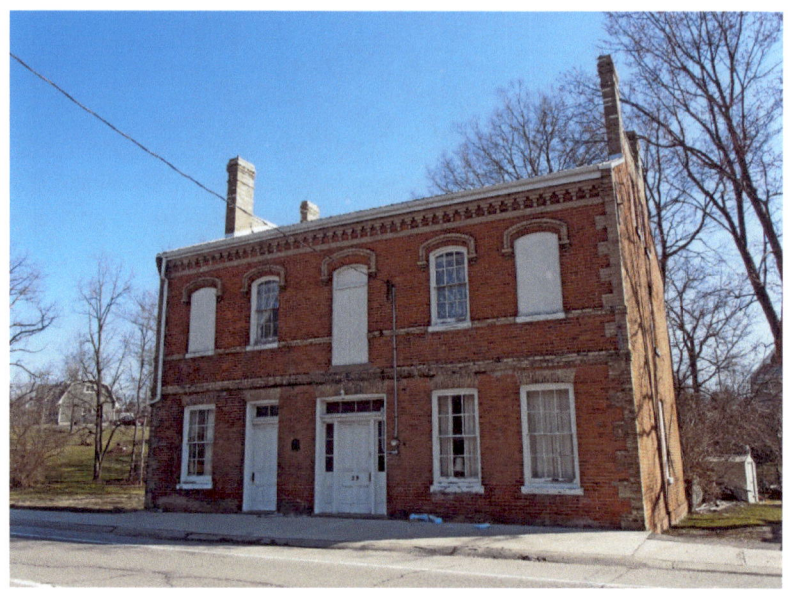

39 Front Street South – The Enniskillen Lodge, formerly the Barber Hotel, was built in 1862 for Mr. Daniel Barber, a prominent local hotelier. Large Georgian style windows, doors, and brick detailing are spaced and designed symmetrically. It has a projected cornice with dentils, Regency four-panel door with sidelights and rectangular transom, hood molds over windows, horizontal banding, and corner quoins.

The Nelles Settlement

After receiving lands on the Grand River in 1784, the Six Nations Indians invited Captain Hendrick Nelles, a Loyalist from the Mohawk Valley, to settle there (present day York) with five of his sons. He and his oldest son Robert established farms in what is now Seneca Township. The Nelles Settlement had about thirty families in 1828.

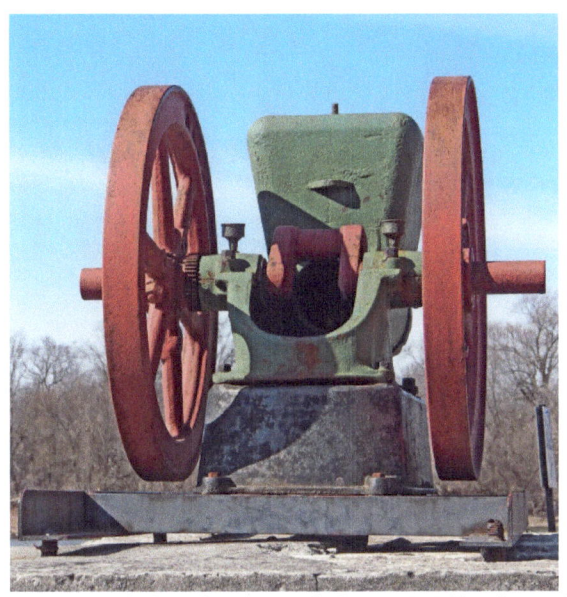

The Davis, Martindale Flour and Grist Mill of York operated for almost a century from the 1820s or 1830s.

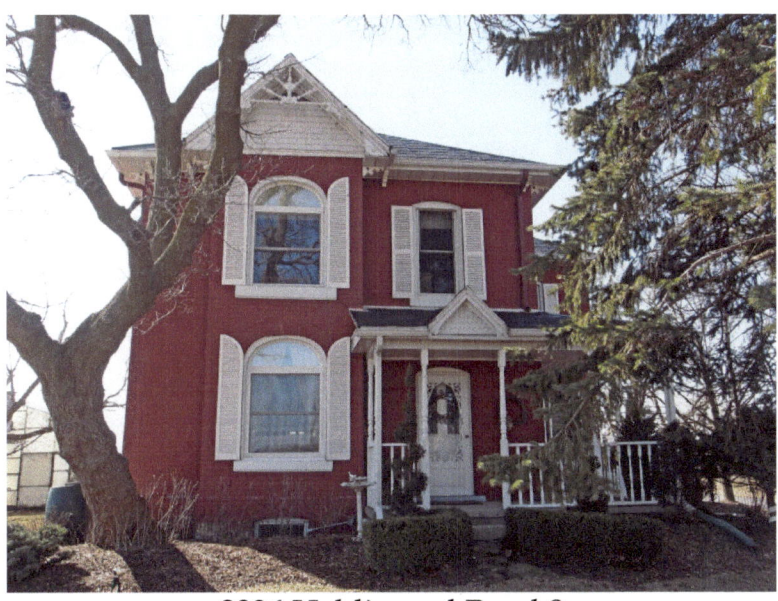

2336 Haldimand Road 9

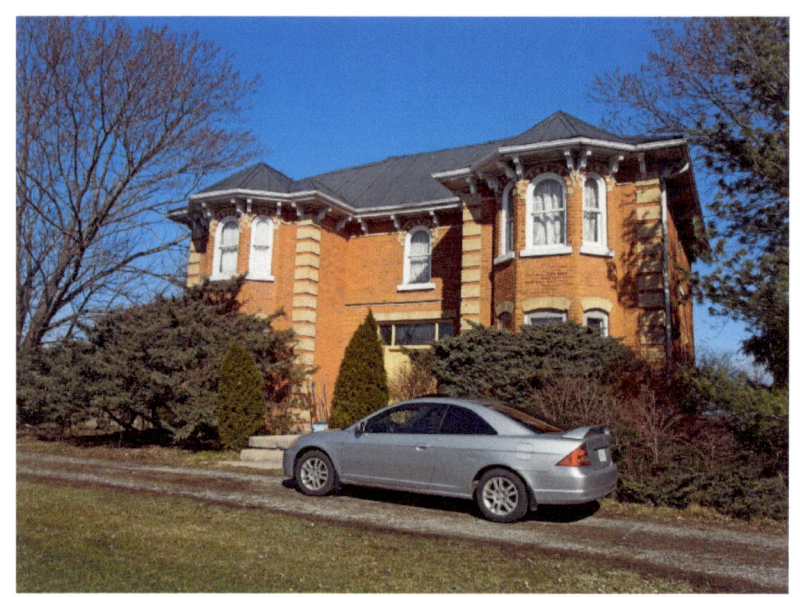
2389 Haldimand Road 9

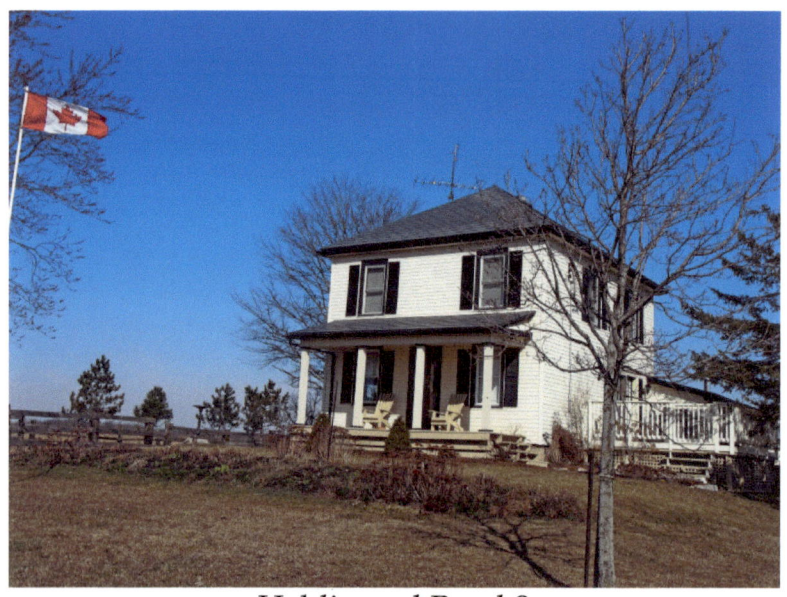
Haldimand Road 9

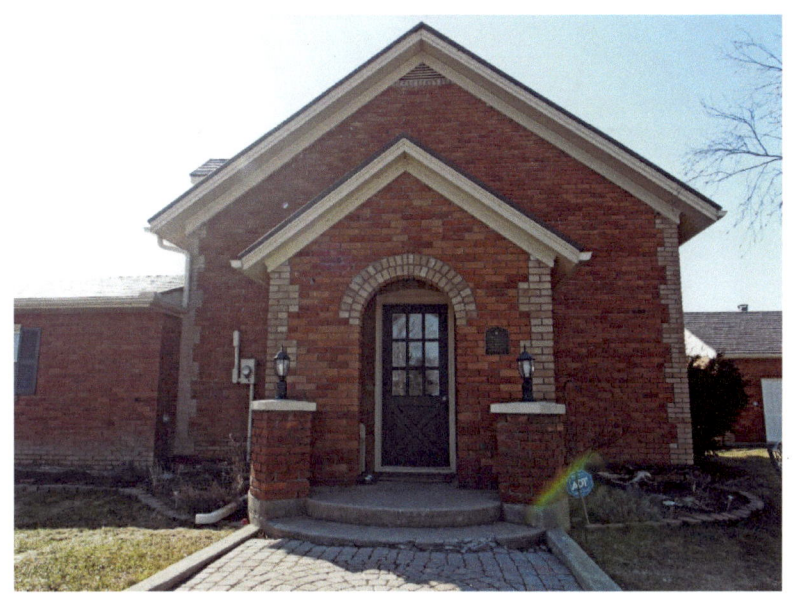

3038 Haldimand Road 9 – S.S. #9 Seneca, Empire School – 1885 (Watson Residence)

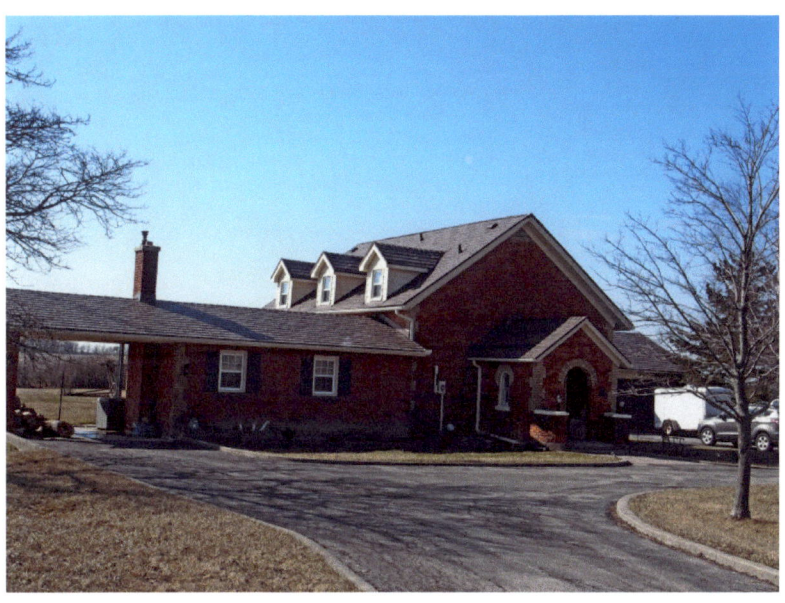

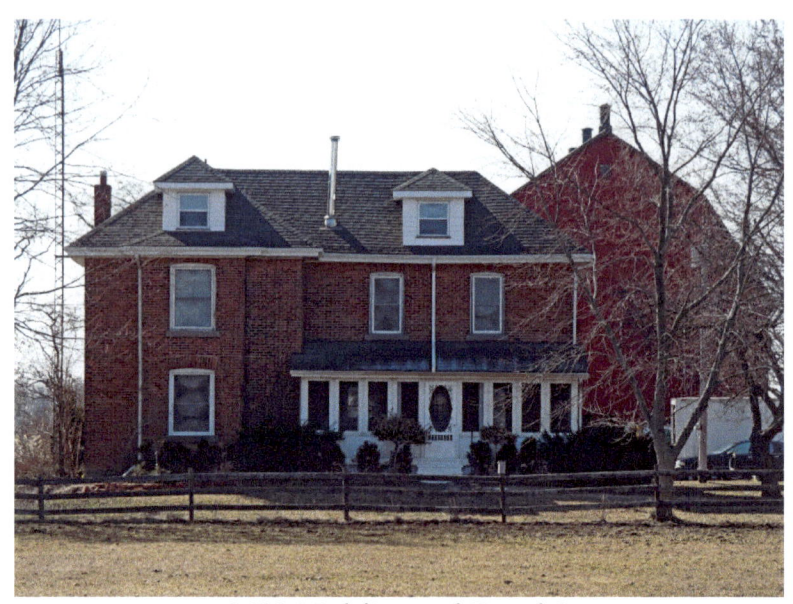

2692 Haldimand Road 9

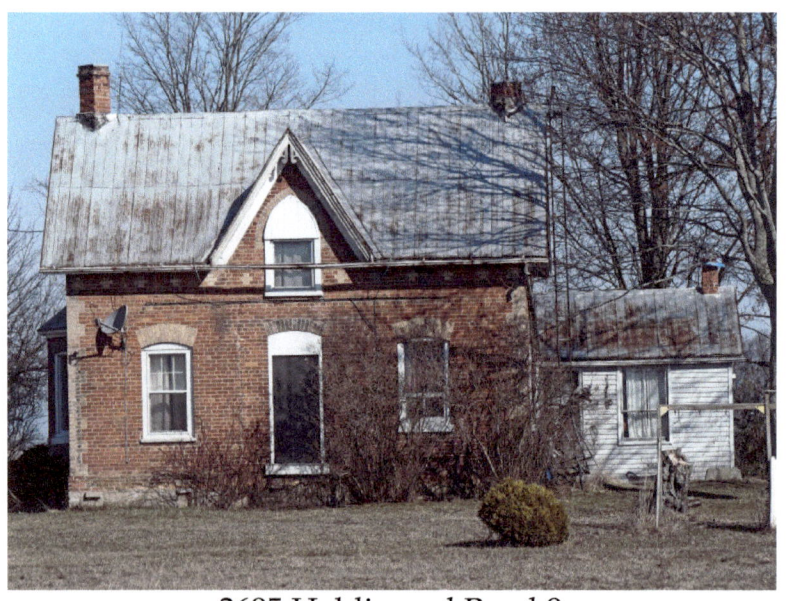

2695 Haldimand Road 9

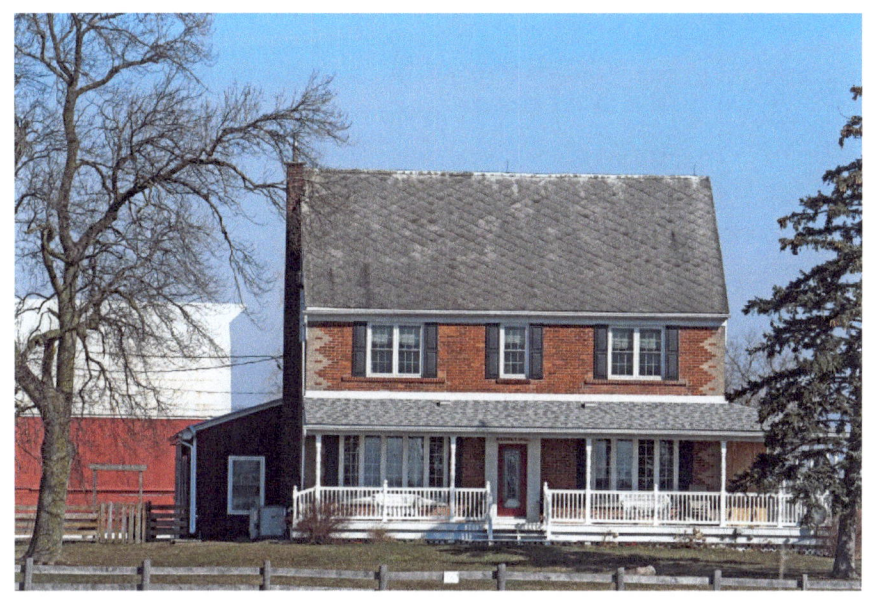

2663 Haldimand Road 9 – Kerney Hill Farm

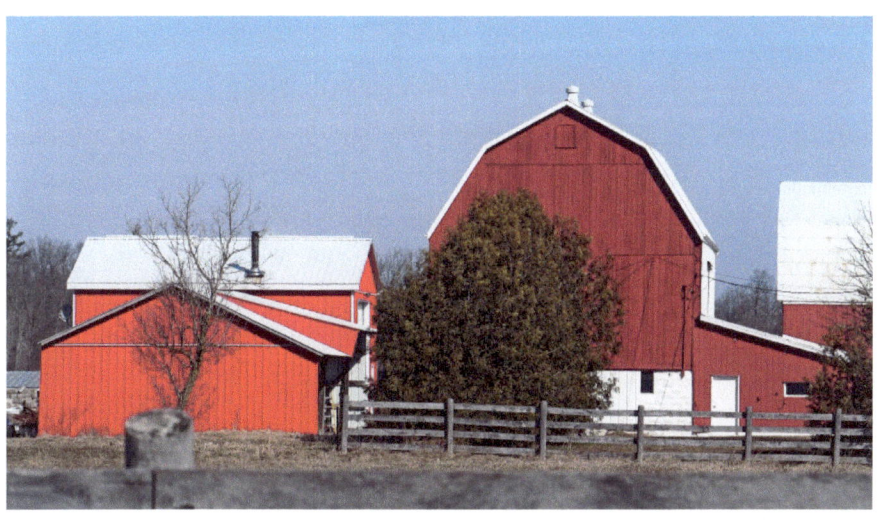

Building Styles

Beaux Arts: Promoters of this style sought to express the classical principles on a grand and imposing scale. Many of the Beaux Arts buildings were banks, post offices, and railway stations. The Ontario Beaux Arts style is eclectic mixing elements of Classical, Renaissance and Baroque. Often the designs have a temple-like façade, porticos with pediments, balustrades, and capitals in many styles.

Classical Revival, 1820-1860 – This style was an analytical, scientific, and dogmatic revival based on intensive studies of Greek and Roman buildings, concerned with the application of Greek plans and proportions to civic buildings. Schools, libraries, government offices, and most other civic buildings were built in the Classical Revival style. The white columned porches of the Classical Revival domestic buildings are identified with the mansions of wealthy land owners in Canada.

Edwardian, 1900-1930 – This style bridges the ornate and elaborate styles of the Victorian era and the simplified styles of the 20th century. Edwardian Classicism provided simple, balanced facades, simple rooflines, dormer windows, large front porches, and smooth brick surfaces. Voussoirs and keystones are used sparingly and are understated. Finials and cresting are absent. Cornice brackets and braces are block-like and openings have flat arches or plain stone lintels.

Garrison - is an architectural style of house, typically two stories with the second story overhanging in the front. The traditional ornamentation is four carved drops (pineapple, strawberry or acorn shape) below the overhang. Garrisons usually have an exterior chimney at the end. Older versions have casement windows with small panes of glass, while later versions have double-hung windows. The second-story windows often are smaller than those on the first floor. Dormers often break through the cornice line.

Georgian, before 1860 – This style began with the British King Georges in the 18th century. These buildings have balanced facades around a central door, medium-pitched gable roofs, and small paned windows.

Gothic Revival, 1830-1890 – These decorative buildings have sharply-pitched gables with highly detailed verge boards, pointed-arch window openings, and dichromatic brickwork. It is a common style in Ontario.

Greek Revival – have gabled or hipped roofs with low pitches. The cornice of the main roof usually has a wide band which represents the entablature of classical Greek architecture consisting of the frieze and the architrave. Greek or Roman columns usually support the porch. The front door is surrounded by sidelights and a rectangular transom and is usually dressed with pilasters, pediments and/or columns.

Italianate, 1850-1900 – A two story rectangular building with a mild hip roof, a projecting frontispiece, and generous eaves with ornate cornice brackets was the basis of the style; often there are large sash windows, quoins, ornate detailing on the windows, belvederes and wraparound verandahs. Italianate commercial buildings often have cast iron cresting and elegant window surrounds.

A **log cabin**, built from logs, was usually one- or 1½-storys constructed with round rather than hewn, or hand-worked, logs, and erected quickly for frontier shelter. Log cabins were built from logs laid horizontally and interlocked on the ends with notches. The cabin was situated to provide sunlight and drainage so the pioneers could cope better with the rigors of frontier life. The pioneers chose old-growth trees that were straight and had few knots and did not need to be hewn to fit well together. Careful notching minimized the size of the gap between the logs and reduced the amount of chinking with sticks and rocks or daubing with mud to fill the gap. The length of one log was the length of one wall.

Neo-Colonial (also Colonial Revival, Georgian Revival or Neo-Georgian) architecture seeks to revive elements of architectural style of American colonial architecture of the period around the Revolutionary War which drew strongly from Georgian architecture of Great Britain. Architecture from the 18th and early 19th centuries in Ontario includes a wide assortment of detailing and ornament applied to a design centered around the fireplace and the source of water. Structures are typically two stories, have a symmetrical front facade with elaborate front doorways, often with decorative crown pediments, fanlights, and sidelights, symmetrical windows flanking the front entrance, often in pairs or threes, and columned porches.

Ontario Cottage - one or one-and-a-half story buildings with a cottage or hip roof. The cottage roof is an equal hip roof where each hip extends to a point in the center of the roof. The hip roof has a long hip in the center. The Ontario Cottage is the vernacular design of the Regency Cottage which generally has a more ornate doorway and a partial or full verandah surrounding it. The roof can have a dormer, a belvedere, and generally two chimneys.

Other Books by Barbara Raue

Coins of Gold
Arrows, Indians and Love
The Life and Times of Barbara
The Cromwell Family Book
Laura Secord Discovered
Daddy Where Are You?

Montana Series
Book 1: Montana Dream
Book 2: Life on the Montana Frontier
Book 3: Montana to Boston and Back
Book 4: Montana Sons Go to War
Book 5: Montana Sons Return from War

Visit Barbara's website to view all of her books
http://barbararaue.ca

Other books on Haldimand County:
Fisherville, Nanticoke and Selkirk Ontario in Colour Photos
Dunnville Ontario Book 1 in Colour Photos
Dunnville Ontario Book 2 and Other Haldimand County towns in Colour Photos
Hagersville Ontario in Colour Photos
Jarvis and Port Dover Ontario in Colour Photos

Barbara is The Authority on Saving Our History One Photo at a Time. She is pursuing her interest in photography and architecture by preserving a record through photos of old buildings from the 1800s and 1900s with their unique architecture. Enjoy the beautiful architecture in the comfort of your living room. Dream about what it was like in those by-gone days. Dream about what it was like to live in a mansion like one of those in this book.

Barbara Raue, a wife, mother and grandmother, is an avid reader and writer. She has researched and compiled several family histories. In 2010, Barbara published her book "Coins of Gold," which celebrates the courageous life of her mother, May Todd. Barbara's second book is a historical fiction "Arrows, Indians and Love" which takes place in Boonesborough, Kentucky during the time of Daniel Boone. In 2013, Barbara published *The Cromwell Family Book* in which she traces her ancestry generations back into Great Britain. Her second novel is called *Laura Secord Discovered,* in which the story of Laura's service during the War of 1812 is shared. Barbara's memoir is titled *Daddy Where Are You?* It tells of her life growing up without a father. Five novels in the Montana Series have been published, *Montana Dream, Life on the Montana Frontier, Montana to Boston and Back, Montana Sons Go to War,* and *Montana Sons Return from War.* The Donaldson series of two novels is available: *Rite of Passage* and *Rite of Marriage.*

This is a link to Barbara's website to view all of her books
http://barbararaue.ca

www.ingramcontent.com/pod-product-compliance
Lightning Source LLC
Chambersburg PA
CBHW040227220526
45473CB00001B/155